AF480871

The 3D Moiré Effect

for Fly-Eye, Lenticular, and Parallax-Barrier Setups

Yitzhak Weissman

Published by

P.O.B 12767, Herzliya 4673324, Israel
Email: **itsikw@pop3dart.com**
Web: **www.pop3dart.com**
Book webpage: **www.pop3dart.com/3d-moire**
The book is being updated with reformulations, extensions, and error fixes. It is being printed on demand, so orders always get the latest revision. The latest revision can also be read online on the book's webpage (subscription required).

Revision 2.2, June 2026

Editions

Description	ISBN
Hardbound print	978-965-598-520-7
Softbound print	978-965-598-521-4

- We had merely struck, at random, a limited part of something
of incalculable extent.

H.P. Lovecraft, "At the Mountains of Madness"

Foreword

Like many of us, I have observed the 3D moiré effect when looking at barriers or fences mounted one behind the other. However, my interest in the scientific aspect of 3D moiré was sparked while practicing lenticular printing and observing the numerous calibration patterns. It became apparent that these patterns displayed a 3D moiré inclined plane. This led me to conduct systematic research on the subject for the past four years, and my findings are detailed in this book. Additionally, I developed software based on the methods and formulas presented in this book to create images and patterns for the 3D moiré effect. The software has been utilized to produce real 3D moiré pictures, providing experimental verification of the underlying formalism.

Despite being known for many years, the 3D moiré effect has only gained significant interest in the past 30 years. During this time, works of art have been created, applications developed, and tools and materials made available. However, to date, there has not been a published systematic study of the 3D moiré effect itself. While testimonials suggest that my predecessors could control certain aspects of the effect, mathematical tools or methods for designing 3D moiré surfaces were not shared, except for a few exceptions in the technical literature. As such, this book presents new and previously unpublished findings in this area.

Probably the most significant result in this book is the sculpting equation for the 3D moiré surface. It is a very powerful tool with far-reaching consequences and is probably published here for the first time. Some readers may wonder what ingenious inspiration has struck me to reveal this equation out of nowhere. One of the great pleasures that mathematics offers to its practitioners is the chance to conceal much hard work behind a concise and polished formulation, leaving the reader astonished. My numerous notes and inscriptions that led to this discovery will wither and fade into oblivion.

The presentation applies to four types of 3D moiré assemblies: fly-eye, lenticular, one-dimensional parallax barrier, and two-dimensional parallax barrier. Although these cases differ in many respects, they share certain fundamental features. Using abstraction and some unconventional notations, it is possible to treat all cases together with a unified formalism. However, after a few attempts, I decided to adopt a hybrid approach in which the presentation is divided into two cases only: one-dimensional and two-dimensional assemblies. The one-dimensional presentation is simpler and is always presented first. The two-dimensional treatment, although more complex, is a straightforward generalization of the corresponding one-dimensional treatment. This format serves a pedagogical purpose: the reader is introduced to the subject with a simpler case, and the following more complex case is presented as a generalization. A separate treatment of each case would have benefited readers interested in only one of the four cases. However, such a presentation would have contained many duplications.

I used numerous diagrams and examples to simplify the presentation, but there are still many unfamiliar objects, tools, and manipulations that require effort and patience to understand. Yet much remains to be uncovered; I leave this task to my successors.

As a personal remark, let me quote an excerpt from a review of my previous book (Weissman, Lenticular Imaging, 2018) which was published on Amazon:

"I have nothing but the deepest respect and admiration for Mr. Yitzhak Weissman (the author). Thank God for men like him, the ones who LIKED math and scoured over countless tables and logarithms to make that concoction that we all hope will transmute the mundane into gold."

Thank you, Simonius, for your outstanding review. It inspired me during my challenging journey.

Yitzhak Weissman

Herzliya, Israel, June 2023

Acknowledgments and credits

I created this book and conducted the research on which it is based entirely on my own. However, it likely would not have been completed and published without the assistance and support of Marek Fragner. His continuing interest and encouragement motivated me to continue. Marek also tested my 3D moiré software and read the manuscript before publication.

I used Microsoft Word to compose the manuscript, Visio to create the drawings, and MathType for the formulas. The book includes a few 3D moiré images as examples, generated in Python. Some of the illustrations of the pseudo-3D effect were done with DAZ Studio.

The front cover picture is based on a drawing by Shorena Tedliashvili (Tedliashvili, 2021).

I used Grammarly to proofread and edit the manuscript.

TABLE OF CONTENTS

1 INTRODUCTION

1.1 The moiré assembly

The moiré effect is a visual phenomenon created by a stack of periodic or repetitive patterns. This phenomenon is called "moiré pattern." We will refer to the moiré stack as "assembly" and to the moiré pattern also as "displayed image."

Moiré assemblies can be divided into two categories:

1. Planar, where all patterns in the assembly are planar and share a common plane,

2. Bulk, where there are at least two patterns in different planes or at least one pattern is on a non-planar surface.

In planar assemblies, the moiré pattern is displayed on the common plane. Such a pattern has only one characteristic: its texture. On the other hand, in bulk assemblies, the moiré pattern is generally displayed on a curved surface and appears in three-dimensional space. Such a pattern is characterized not only by its texture but also by its 3D geometry. The visual effect of moiré bulk assemblies will be called the "3D moiré effect," and it is the subject of the present book.

Throughout this book, we will assume that the assembly is infinite. In infinite assemblies, there are no edge effects, which simplifies the presentation.

1.2 The moiré effect in planar assemblies

Planar assemblies give rise to the familiar moiré effect (Moiré pattern, 2023), (Amidror, 2009). Figure 1 shows an example of a moiré planar assembly with two patterns, one serving as a background and the other as a mask. For the moiré pattern to appear, the mask must contain transparent regions that allow parts of the background pattern to be seen.

The background pattern can be fully opaque, so the moiré pattern is visible only from the front. However, it may also contain transparent regions as the mask. In such a case, the moiré effect can be observed from both the front and the back. When the assembly is observed from the back, the patterns change their roles: the mask becomes the background, and the background becomes the mask.

The moiré effect manifests as a new pattern created by the interaction between the mask and the background. The moiré pattern graphics are related to the geometry of the original patterns but often exhibit unexpected features. These characteristics of the moiré pattern create curiosity and attract attention. Therefore, kits with various pattern pairs are popular for experimenting and playing with the moiré effect.

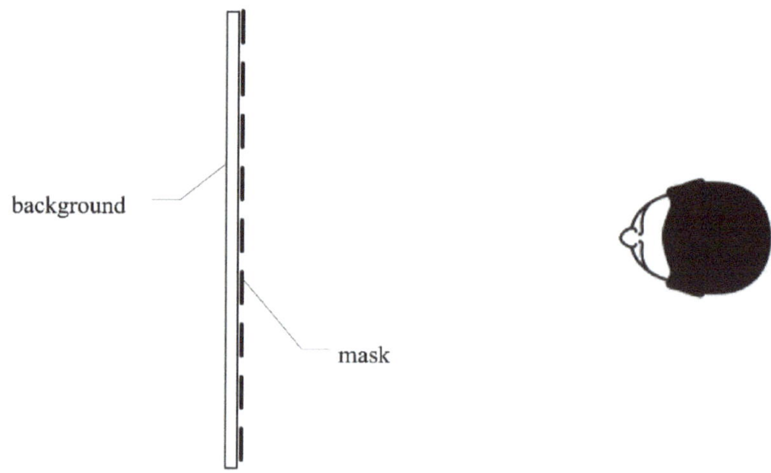

Figure 1:   A simple planar moiré assembly

An example of the moiré effect with a mask and background is shown in Figure 2 and Figure 3. Both pictures are prints of the same image: a lattice of black dots. However, the mask is printed on a transparent medium, and the background is on brown paper. A stack of these patterns is shown in Figure 3. The two patterns are slightly rotated with respect to each other, giving rise to the familiar moiré effect.

The moiré scenario in this case comprises three images: the background, the mask, and the moiré pattern. The first two are printed on a tangible medium; the third is virtual and exists only as an interaction of the first two. It is very sensitive to their relative displacement and rotation. This characteristic led to many applications of the moiré effect in metrology (Kafri & Glatt, 1989). Most of the research on the moiré effect is devoted to the study of displayed moiré patterns in planar assemblies (Amidror, 2009).

Figure 2:   Two patterns used for the moiré effect. Left: background, right: mask

Figure 3:   Stack of the pictures of Figure 2, with the mask in front

1.3   The 3D moiré effect

At the time of the writing of this book, the popular AI chatbot ChatGPT gave the following description of the 3D moiré phenomenon:

"3D moiré is a visual phenomenon where two or more patterns with slightly different three-dimensional structures overlap, producing a new pattern with a distinct visual effect. This effect is caused by interference between the individual patterns, which creates regions of constructive and destructive interference. The resulting pattern can appear to move and vibrate, depending on the viewer's point of view, and can be used to create interesting and dynamic visual effects in art and design."

This describes the visual features of the effect well but fails to explicitly refer to its 3D properties. This book will treat a special case in which there are only two planar patterns (with the exception of Chapter 11) and focus on the 3D characteristics of the "resulting pattern." Even this special case can yield a wealth of astonishing visual effects.

Figure 4 shows a bulk moiré assembly: the two patterns are in two different (but parallel) planes (Saveljev, 2023).

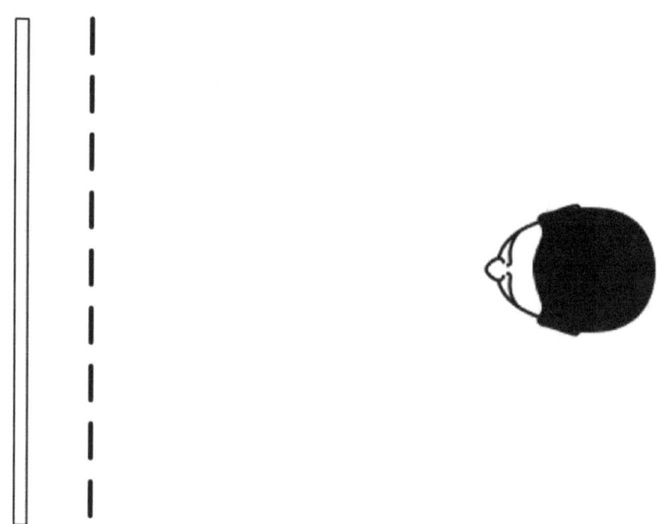

Figure 4:   A bulk moiré assembly

In the planar moiré setup, the moiré pattern appears in the common plane of the two original patterns. In the bulk assembly, there are also two patterns, but they do not share a common plane. This raises the questions: where does the moiré pattern appear in such circumstances? Does it appear in the mask plane or the background plane, or maybe in an entirely different plane? To cope with these questions, let us investigate the viewing scenario of Figure 4 in a little more detail.

The moiré pattern is created because the mask obscures certain areas in the background. To understand its action in the bulk setup, the mask should be separated into two entities: the obscuring mask and the sampling mask. The obscuring mask is the actual mask. The sampling mask is a virtual object; it is the projection of the obscuring mask on the background plane, with the viewing point serving as the projection center. This is shown in Figure 5, where one of the observer's eyes was chosen as the viewing point.

The background regions seen from a given viewing point are determined by the sampling mask, whose position and geometry depend on this point. Therefore, each observer's eye will be exposed to a different moiré pattern. If certain conditions are fulfilled, this will create a 3D illusion, and the moiré pattern may appear on a certain surface in space. The assembly geometry and the background image graphics determine the location and geometry of this surface.

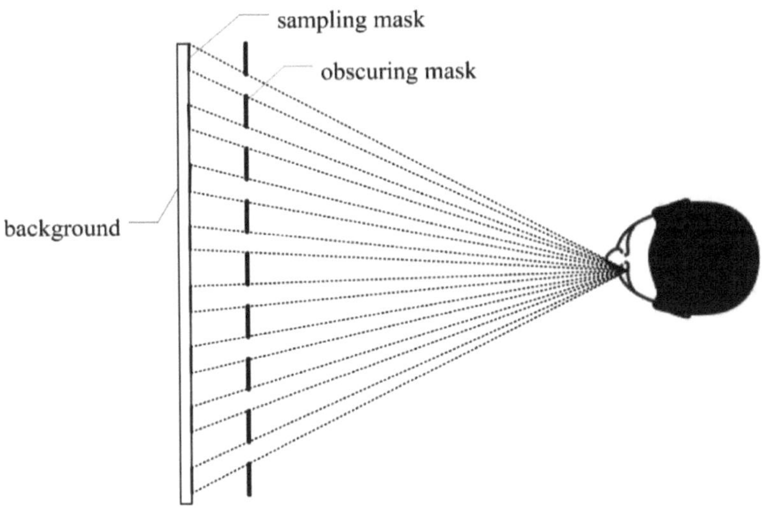

Figure 5:   Projection of the front pattern on the back pattern

Barriers or parapets are often constructed from periodic patterns. In some instances, it is possible to view two such structures, one behind the other. The 3D moiré pattern appears spontaneously in such circumstances; therefore, it is a relatively familiar phenomenon. With the advent of lenslet array sheets, practitioners have noted the striking visual appeal of the 3D moiré effect and started to exploit it commercially in signage and art.

1.4   The 3D moiré law

In 2019, the author came upon a law that quantitatively predicts the location of the moiré pattern created by viewing two periodic patterns deposited on two parallel planes, with the back pattern being a projection of the front one (Weissman, The 3D moiré law, 2019). The 3D moiré law states that the displayed moiré pattern will appear on a plane parallel to the mask plane and passing through the projection point. Figure 6 illustrates this using familiar objects: a point light source and cast shadows. However, the 3D moiré law is not limited to this scenario and is more general, as will be shown below. The law demonstrates that the displayed moiré pattern may appear anywhere in space, and its position is controlled by the position of the projection point (the point light source in this case). In particular, if the projection point is at infinity, the shadow pattern becomes identical to the mask, and the displayed image appears at infinity.

In the present nomenclature, the front pattern in Figure 6 serves as the mask, and its cast shadows serve as the background image. The shadow pattern is obtained from the mask by a projection transformation, with the point light source as the projection point.

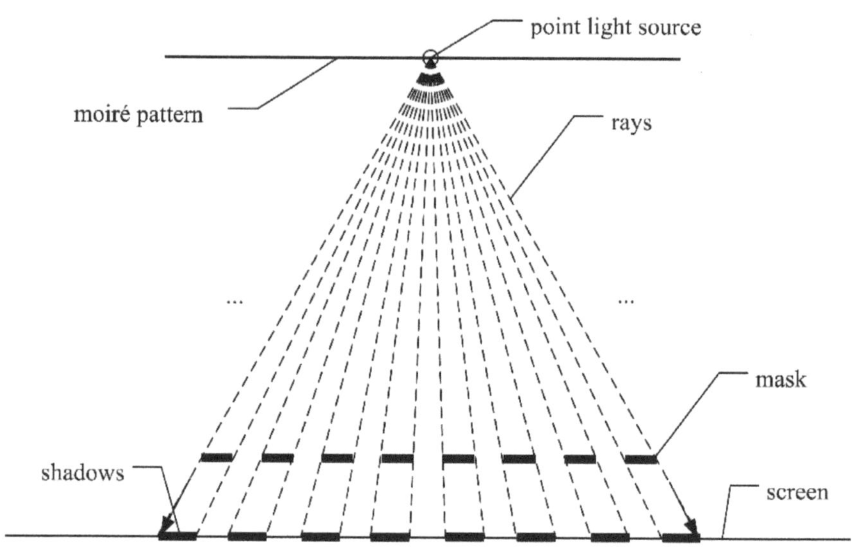

Figure 6:   An illustration of the 3D moiré law (Weissman, The 3D moiré law, 2019)

The scenario shown in Figure 6 can be generalized to a case in which the moiré pattern is displayed behind the screen. This generalization is achieved by observing that, optically, a point light source can be a focal point of a converging beam, and that a focal point can replace the light point source as the projection point. If we let the focal point be behind the screen, we obtain the scenario shown in Figure 7. In this case, the moiré pattern is displayed behind the screen.

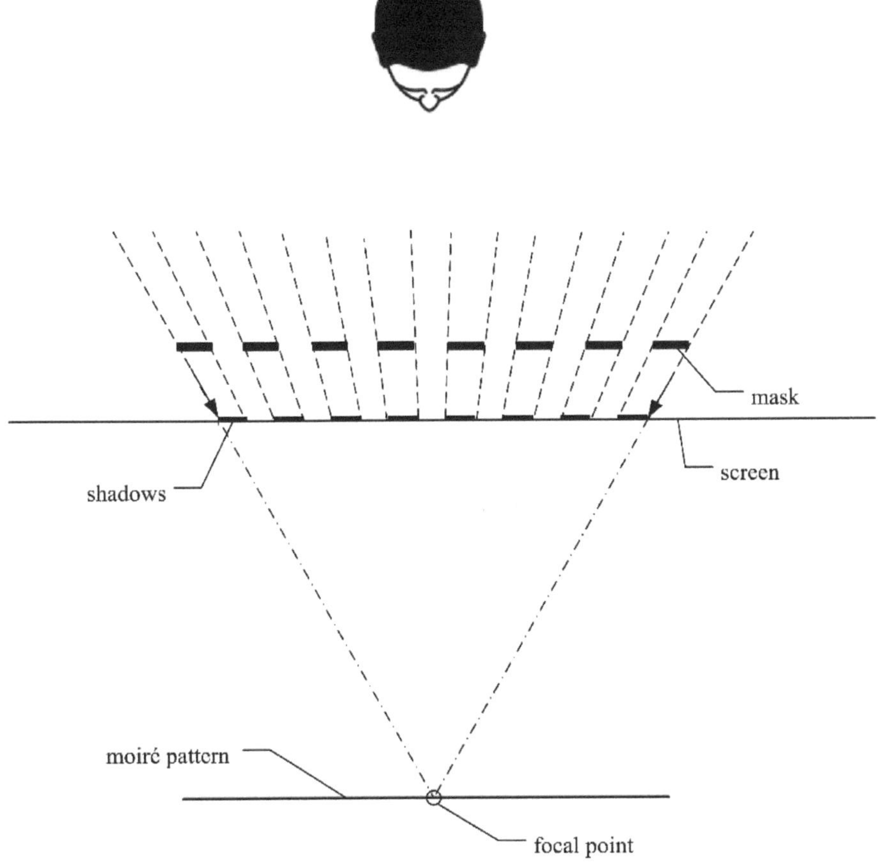

Figure 7:   An illustration of the 3D moiré law with a moiré pattern displayed behind the screen

1.5   Moiré pattern sculpting

The 3D moiré law can be used to construct moiré assemblies that display the 3D moiré pattern on an arbitrarily specified 3D surface. We will illustrate this using a simple photographic setup, shown in Figure 8.

In this setup, the screen is replaced with a photographic plate that can permanently record the mask shadows. Imagine that this plate is divided into many area elements, so that each can be exposed by a special exposure assembly containing a variable zoom lens and an exposure aperture. The exposure assembly can be moved parallel to the mask plane, and during this motion, the exposure aperture is kept close to this plane. The exposure assembly is illuminated by a parallel beam of light, which the lens focuses onto a specified virtual surface. A special mechanism (not shown) guarantees that the focal point follows the virtual surface as the exposure assembly moves. The exposure aperture is designed to fit the area elements of the photographic plate.

The photographic plate is exposed by moving the exposure assembly from one area element to another and exposing it. This is repeated until all area elements are exposed. Note that the recorded shadow pattern in each area element is a projected shadow of the mask with a projection point located on the specified virtual surface above it.

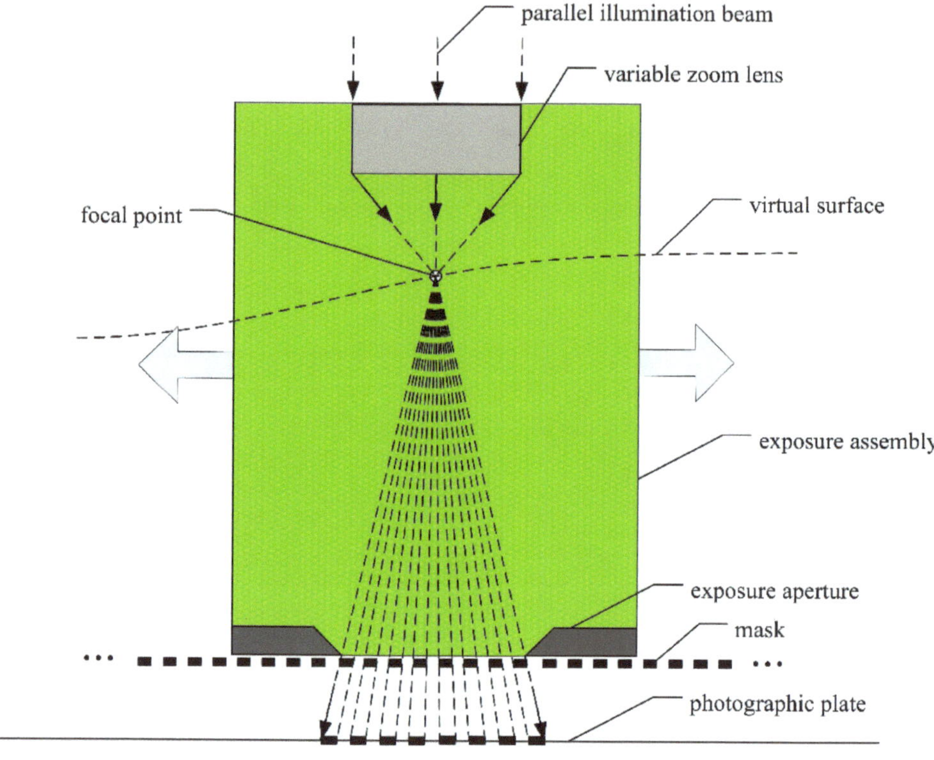

Figure 8   Photographic method for sculpting the moiré surface

To view the 3D moiré pattern, the photographic plate is developed to display the recorded composite shadow pattern. The viewing scenario is shown in Figure 9. The mask is the same as the one used for the exposure, and its distance from the developed plate is the same as in the exposure procedure. Applying the 3D moiré law to each surface element, we conclude that its moiré pattern will be displayed on the corresponding surface element on the virtual surface. If the area elements are sufficiently small, the 3D moiré pattern will be smoothly displayed on the specified surface, as shown in Figure 9.

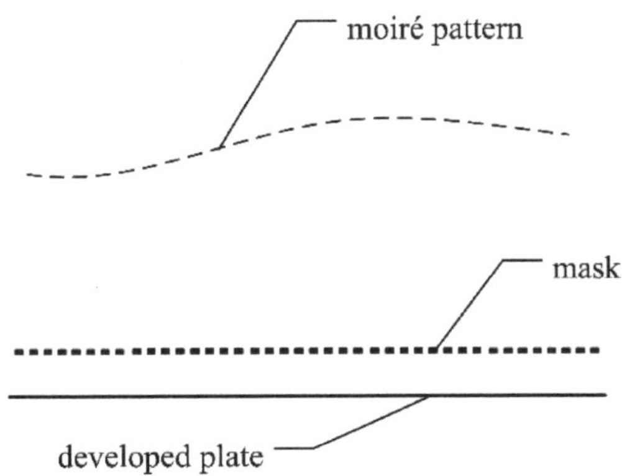

Figure 9:   Viewing the 3D moiré pattern

The compound shadow pattern on the developed plate is related to the mask pattern by a certain plane-to-plane transformation. This transformation depends on the specified surface and the gap between the mask and the plate planes. In what follows, mathematical tools for deriving this transformation are presented.

1.6   The 3D moiré effect: a review

Parallax barrier (Parallax barrier, 2022), is a well-known technique for 3D stereoscopic displays. The 3D parallax barrier stereoscopic setup scenario is identical to the one shown in Figure 4, except that the background pattern is not a periodic image. Instead, it is a special image created by a process called "interlacing" from a pair of stereo images. Parallax barrier setups were the first to be investigated in the context of the 3D moiré effect.

On May 21, 1974, Robert Eaves was awarded a patent on a concept based on Figure 4 (USA Patent No. 3,811,213, 1974). Eaves patterns were made of dots, and he focused on animated displays in which the mask is movable relative to the background. However, a static arrangement exhibiting a 3D moiré pattern is described, although not claimed: *"... the depth illusion is accomplished with a single* (transparent, YW) *sheet ... having related dot patterns applied to opposed parallel surfaces..."* In this case, the sheet thickness defines the gap between the mask and the background. The background is described as a pattern comprising a plurality of sections of dot patterns with different frequencies.

Eaves refers in his patent to using the moiré effect with lenticular lenses. He dismisses this method, saying that *"... these lenticular devices often result in wavy or blurred images and are often uncomfortable for the observer to view."* The lenticular and fly-eye technologies have made significant improvements since then. Nowadays, moiré assemblies with lenslet arrays are much superior in visual quality to parallax barrier moiré assemblies.

Benny Pesach has also applied for a patent on a concept based on Figure 4 (Pesach, 1997). Here is a citation of his patent application abstract:

"Apparatus and method for producing a depth illusion of continuous three-dimensional objects using the Moiré effect is presented. The apparatus includes at least two surfaces separated by a small distance, one of which surfaces is a transparent sheet imprinted with vertical or nearly vertical, line patterns with slowly varying period in a horizontal direction, and the other is imprinted with a color or black and white horizontally almost periodic pattern related to the other surface pattern in such a way that the combination of both patterns produces a Moiré pattern that creates a depth illusion in the observer's mind."

Compared to Eaves, Pesach's innovation lies in the concept of a "slowly varying period" in the background pattern. This is essentially a continuous warping of the periodic background image and can result in 3D moiré sculpting. Actually, Pesach demonstrated 3D moiré sculpting of a sphere. However, neither Pesach nor Eaves disclose any formulas or algorithms for controlling the geometry of the 3D moiré pattern.

Joe Huck has rediscovered the 3D moiré effect and was fascinated by its artistic appeal. Here is a citation from Huck's blog (Huck, 2002):

"What I've discovered (more correctly, rediscovered, for it's been known for the better part of a century or more) and studied extensively is the fact that patterns created from two screens in angular alignment but with a slight separation between them, will appear to float in space either in front of or behind the interacting screens, at a position determined by the screens' rulings and the distance between them. The floating moiré space thus created and the patterns that inhabit and define it, like the

normal 3D space we inhabit, are delimited by a set of mathematical rules that can be used to predict how certain configurations will appear. "

This citation suggests that Huck was aware that certain mathematical rules could predict the position of the 3D moiré patterns. But, like his predecessors, Eaves and Pesach, he did not share these rules.

Huck's motivation in exploring the 3D moiré effect was artistic. He has discovered that imaging is possible with the parallax barrier method if the width of the transparent regions in the mask is made much smaller compared to the opaque areas:

"Another feature of moiré patterns that is essential to my work, is the fact that a screen made of repeated or similar images will create a pattern composed of the same (but much enlarged) images, if it is made to interact with a screen whose elements consist of the smallest openings possible for the particular type of screen: dots or pinhole openings for rectilinear screens and lines or slits for linear screens."

Unfortunately, reducing the size of the transparent regions leads to darker images. This imposes a critical tradeoff between displayed image resolution and brightness (see below Chapter 10) and limits the use of the parallax barrier method for art. Nevertheless, Huck succeeded in producing remarkable art with this method and is entitled to recognition as a pioneer of 3D moiré art. Unfortunately, Huck's artworks cannot be found, so we do not know what they looked like.

Keita Nagasaki and Yue Bao have investigated an experimental setup that displays a 3D moiré pattern with a variable depth (Nagasaki & Bao, 2008). The system is also based on the diagram of Figure 4, except that the background pattern was projected on the backplane by a projector with a zoom lens. Variation in the projector zoom affects the background pattern pitch. This, in turn, modifies the position of the 3D moiré pattern, as suggested by the 3D moiré law (Figure 6). In their study, Nagasaki & Rao published a formula for the location of the 3D moiré pattern in space as a function of the parameters of the experimental setup. The 3D moiré assembly was also investigated by Saveljev (Saveljev, 2023).

With the advent of printing technology, it became possible to produce 3D moiré assemblies by printing. In 2012, the Grapac company (Grapac Japan, 2023) introduced a printing service for cards exhibiting the 3D moiré effect based on fly-eye lenses. This technology was branded HALS (**H**oneycomb **A**rray **L**ens **S**heet) (HALS, 2023).

Recently, it became possible to print micro-lens arrays with inkjet printers (Cox, Chen, & Hayes, 2001). In 2014, Popims Lens Printer (Popims Lens Printer, 2023) and SwissQPrint (SwissQPrint, 2023) companies commercialized this technique with UV flat-bed inkjet printers. SwissQPrint branded the tools for making 3D moiré assemblies by inkjet printing under the name Droptix (Droptix, 2023).

2 BASIC CONCEPTS

2.1   The fundamental objects of moiré assemblies

The diagram in Figure 10 illustrates the fundamental components used in bulk moiré assemblies with two patterns. While the nature of these components may vary between different assemblies, they are present in all such assemblies.

The moiré assembly is enclosed in Figure 10 in a dash-dotted line rectangle. It is represented by two planes: the front plane and the backplane. The planes are parallel to each other and are separated by the assembly gap t. The backplane contains an image, and the front plane a certain periodic structure, to be discussed below.

The displayed image, in general, will appear somewhere in space. Figure 10 suggests that the displayed image is planar, but in general, it can have arbitrary geometry. In this book, we will use V and H to denote the distances from the assembly front plane to the viewing point and the displayed image (if it is planar), respectively.

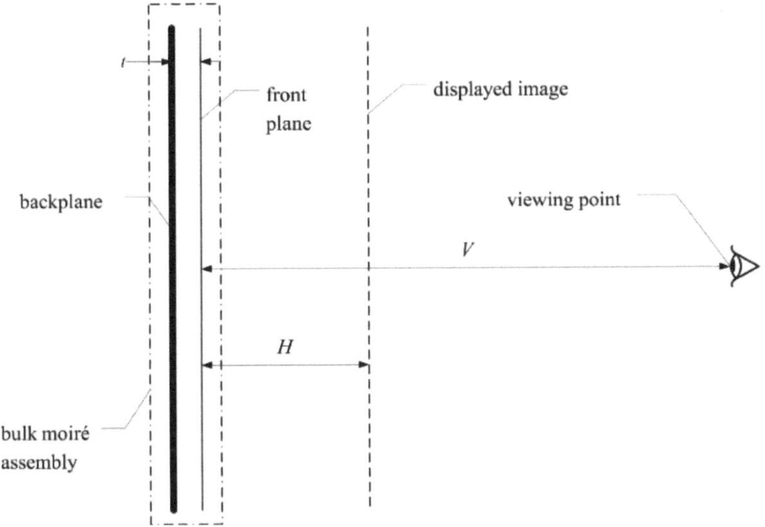

Figure 10:   The fundamental geometry of a bulk moiré assembly and its viewing scenario

Analytical geometry tools will often be used for the analysis. To apply these tools, it is necessary to define a coordinate system. A Cartesian coordinate system for the assembly is defined in Figure 11. The origin of the system is on the backplane, and the z axis is perpendicular to it. The backplane coordinates will be also denoted often by u and v.

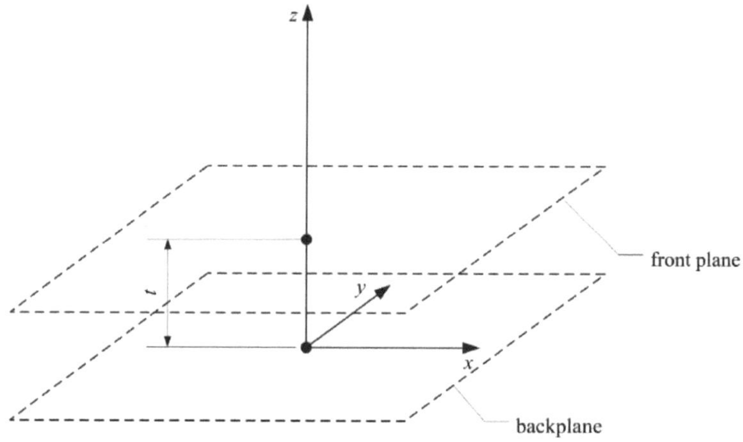

Figure 11:   Coordinates for the bulk moiré assembly

2.2   The classification of bulk moiré assemblies

The mechanism that forms the displayed image divides the bulk moiré assemblies into two categories:

- Parallax barrier,

- Optical.

In parallax barrier assemblies, the front plane contains a mask. The mask pattern has transparent regions that reveal specific parts of the background image. The background image is printed on a transparent or opaque medium. Parallax barrier pictures with a semi-transparent background pattern can also be viewed from behind.

Optical moiré assemblies contain a lenslet (or micro-lens) array sheet, and the displayed image is formed by an optical mechanism. The background image is normally opaque. Optical assemblies can be viewed only from the front.

Assemblies will also be categorized as either one-dimensional (1D) or two-dimensional (2D). This classification is independent of the image-forming classification; therefore, we will treat four categories of bulk moiré assemblies.

One-dimensional and two-dimensional optical assemblies are called "lenticular" and "fly-eye," respectively. There are no common names for parallax barrier assemblies, so we will call them one and two-dimensional parallax barrier (PB1D and PB2D, respectively). The full classification of bulk moiré assemblies is shown in Table 1.

Table 1:   *Classification of bulk moiré assemblies*

Classification	Optical	Parallax barrier
One-dimensional	Lenticular	PB1D
Two-dimensional	Fly-eye	PB2D

2.3   Images

Mathematically, an image is a vector function defined on a rectangle. The number of components in the image function depends on the image type. The most common images, their numbers of components, and their descriptions are listed in Table 2.

Table 2:   *Image types and their functions components*

Image type	No. of components of the image function	Components
Black and white	One	Grey level
Color	Three	Color (RGB)
Color with transparency	Four	Color (RGB) and alpha channel

The image function depends on two arguments: the two coordinates of an image point (Pratt, 1991).

Let I denote an image function. An image is said to be periodic in one dimension if there is a vector $a \neq 0$ such that

$$I(x+a) = I(x) \tag{2.1}$$

for any image point x. The vector a is an image basis vector, and its magnitude $|a|$ is an image period. Throughout this book, the coordinate axes of one-dimensional periodic images will always be aligned so that the basis vector is parallel to the x axis. This convention allows us to refer to the basis vector as a scalar.

A periodic image in one dimension can be created by tiling a plane with identical cells along the x-axis, where each cell extends to both $+\infty$ and $-\infty$ in the direction of the y-axis, and its x cross-section width for any given y coordinate is constant. This constant is the image period. An infinite vertical band of width equal to the image period is a simple example of a cell.

An image is periodic in two dimensions if there are two non-parallel vectors a and b, such that

$$I(x+a) = I(x), \text{ and } I(x+b) = I(x) \tag{2.2}$$

for all x. Vectors a and b are basis vectors of the image. The vectors

$$P_{k,l} = ka + lb \tag{2.3}$$

where k and l are integers, are called "image vectors."

The image dimensionality is generally not unique, and neither are the basis vectors. Since (2.2) is a special case of (2.1), it follows that a two-dimensional image is also one-dimensional. It is also easy to prove that if a is a basis vector, so is $2a$. It is constructive to keep these facts in mind, but they do not interfere with our analysis, which is based on existence rather than on uniqueness.

2.4   Grids and lattices

A grid is a set of equidistant parallel lines. Let us assume that the gridlines are parallel to the y axis, so their equations are $x = x_k$, where $\{x_k\}$ is a set of points on the x-axis which are called "grid coordinates." The grid coordinates are given by

$$x_k = x_0 + kd,$$

where x_0 is the grid origin, k is an integer, and d is the grid step.

A lattice is a set of points $\{x_{k,l}\}$ with coordinates

$$x_{k,l} = x_{0,0} + ke + lf , \tag{2.4}$$

where $x_{0,0}$ is the lattice origin, and k, l are integers. The vectors e and f are the basis vectors of the lattice.

2.5   Front plane structures

The front plane structure is an important auxiliary tool for both the analysis and the synthesis of the 3D moiré effect. This structure is an array of identical structure units. Both the structure and the structure units are virtual objects.

A structure unit comprises two geometrical objects: a cell and a center object. The cell is a planar geometric shape, which can be a polygon or an infinite band. The center object is either a point or a line. The center object is normally located at the cell's center, but this is not required. The structure's cells form a tiling (Tessalation, 2023) of the front plane.

In this book we limit ourselves to 1D assemblies whose cells are vertical bands of a constant width extending to infinity. The center objects of such cells are lines parallel to the cell's boundary. In 1D assemblies, the coordinate system (Figure 11) will be aligned so that the y axis is parallel to the center lines.

The 1D structure can be created by aligning the structure unit so that its centerline is parallel to the y-axis, duplicating it and translating the duplication parallel to the x-axis by kd for all integer k, where d is the cell's width. Such a structure is periodic with a basis vector

$$\boldsymbol{a} = [d, 0].$$

For integer k, the vectors

$$\boldsymbol{s}_k = [kd, 0]$$

will be called "structure vectors." A 1D structure is shown schematically in Figure 12.

The cells of a 2D assembly are finite polygons, and the center objects are points. The 2D structure possesses two basis vectors $\boldsymbol{a}$ and $\boldsymbol{b}$, and structure vectors

$$\boldsymbol{s}_{k,l} = k\boldsymbol{a} + l\boldsymbol{b}$$

for all integers k, l. The 2D structure is created by duplicating and shifting the structure unit by all structure vectors. The structure unit cell and the structure vectors must be such that the structure cells form a tiling of the front plane without gaps or overlaps. The 2D structure is periodic in two dimensions.

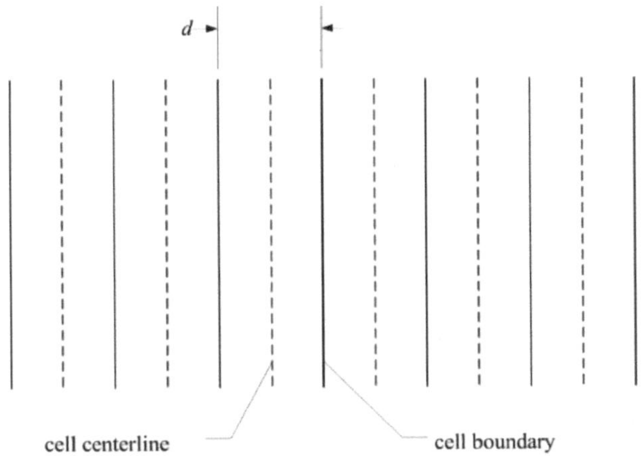

Figure 12:   Front plane structure in a 1D assembly

A 2D structure is distinguished from a 1D structure by the fact that the center objects of a 1D structure form a grid, whereas the center objects of a 2D structure form a lattice. An example of a 2D assembly structure with square cells is shown in Figure 13. The structure basis vectors in this case are

$$\boldsymbol{a} = (d, 0), \quad \boldsymbol{b} = (0, d).$$

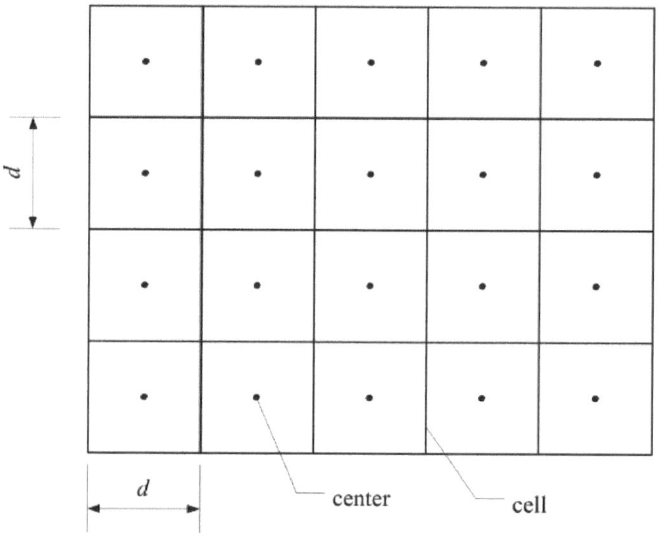

Figure 13: Front plane structure of a square 2D assembly

The basis vectors are, in general, not orthogonal, and therefore cannot be chosen to be simultaneously parallel to the coordinate axes.

2.6 Operator notation

We will often use operators acting on objects in mathematical equations. The following notation will be used to represent this action:

$$\boldsymbol{P} = G(a_1, a_2, ..., a_n)\{\boldsymbol{Q}\}.$$

In this example, G is an operator that depends on a set of parameters $a_1, a_2, ..., a_n$, and $\boldsymbol{P}$ and $\boldsymbol{Q}$ are the output and input objects, respectively.

3 PROJECTION TRANSFORMATIONS

3.1 General

This book often uses projection transformations in three-dimensional space (3D projection, 2022). Such a projection operation requires three objects:

1. Projection point,
2. Projected object,
3. Projection surface.

Generally, the projected object and the projection surface can have arbitrary shapes. Here, the projected object will always lie in the assembly front plane. Except for Chapter 11, the projection surface will be the assembly back plane. The projected objects that will be considered are points, grids, lattices, and images. All these objects will lie in the object plane.

3.2 Projection transformation from the front to the back plane

The projection scenario is shown in Figure 14. Point B serves as the projection point. Points P and P' are a point on the front plane and its projection on the backplane, respectively:

$$P = \left[P_x, P_y, t \right],$$
$$P' = \left[P'_x, P'_y, 0 \right].$$

Line BO is perpendicular to both planes. It is evident that triangles $\triangle BOP$ and $\triangle BO'P'$ are similar. Therefore

$$P' - O' = \alpha_h (P - O), \tag{3.1}$$

where α_h is the projection constant:

$$\alpha_h = 1 + \frac{1}{h}, \tag{3.2}$$

and h is the normalized projection distance:

$$h = \frac{H}{t}. \tag{3.3}$$

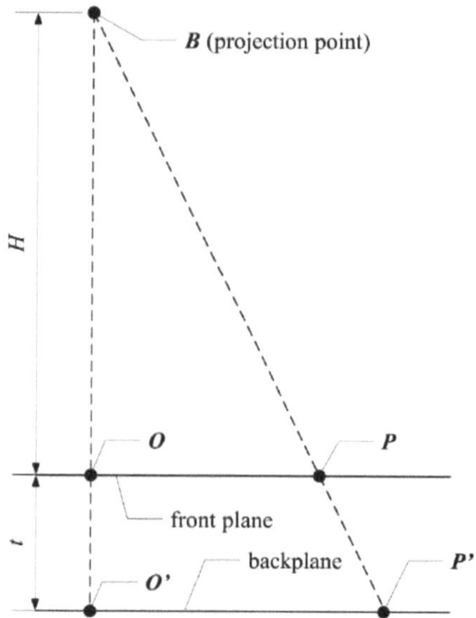

Figure 14:   Projection of a point

The quantity H may be signed. In Figure 14, H is positive. When the projection point is behind the front plane, the value of H is negative. Equation (3.1) is valid for both positive and negative H.

If the projection point is located at infinity, then

$$\boldsymbol{P}' = \left[P_x,\ P_y,\ 0 \right].$$
(3.4)

The projection is undefined for $h = 0$, because there is no projected point in this case. Typically, t is much smaller than $|H|$, so $\alpha_h \approx 1$.

Here, we will consider projections from the front plane to the backplane only. These planes are parallel, and according to Figure 11, they are also parallel to the xy plane. Therefore, in each plane, the z coordinate is constant and can be dropped. The resulting points will be called "planar." We will denote the planar points in the front and back planes by $\boldsymbol{x}$ and $\boldsymbol{u}$, respectively.

The planar points corresponding to $\boldsymbol{P'}$, $\boldsymbol{O'}$, $\boldsymbol{P}$, and $\boldsymbol{O}$ are

$$\boldsymbol{x} = \left[P_x, P_y \right], \quad \boldsymbol{o} = \boldsymbol{o}' = \left[O_x, O_y \right], \quad \boldsymbol{u} = \left[P'_x, P'_y \right]$$
(3.5)

Since the planes are parallel, (3.1) is also valid for the planar coordinates, namely

$$\boldsymbol{u} - \boldsymbol{o} = \alpha_h \left(\boldsymbol{x} - \boldsymbol{o} \right),$$
(3.6)

where we have used the fact that $o = o'$. Equation (3.6) defines a transformation from the front plane to the backplane:

$$u(x) = \alpha_h (x - o) + o = \alpha_h x - \frac{o}{h}. \tag{3.7}$$

The inverse transformation is

$$x(u) = \alpha_h^{-1}(u - o) + o = \frac{u}{\alpha_h} + \frac{o}{1+h}. \tag{3.8}$$

Equations (3.7) and (3.8) may be regarded as a coordinate transformation. A transformation of coordinates modifies the image function, creating a new image. Such image transformation is called "warping" (Wolberg, 1990). A projection transformation is a special case of warping.

Let us now consider a projection of an image $\Phi(x)$ that is deposited on the front surface. According to (3.8) the projected image $\Phi'(u)$ on the backplane is given by

$$\Phi'(u) = \Phi\left[\frac{u}{\alpha_h} + \frac{o}{1+h}\right]. \tag{3.9}$$

The projected image is derived from the original image by a uniform scaling transformation (Scaling, 2022) with the scaling factor α_h^{-1}, and a translation.

3.3   Displacement of the projected point

We will often use the viewing point of the assembly as the projection point and investigate the dynamics of the displayed image in response to the observer's movement. We will limit ourselves to scenarios in which the viewing point is confined to move on a plane parallel to the assembly. In such scenarios, the projected images from the front to the back plane will be scaled by the same factor, and the only difference between them will be a translation.

Let us consider two viewing points that are at the same distance H from the front plane:

$$O_1 = \left[O_{1x}, O_{1y}, H\right], \quad O_2 = \left[O_{2x}, O_{2y}, H\right].$$

Since the z coordinate is the same, we can use the planar coordinates instead:

$$o_1 = \left[O_{1x}, O_{1y}\right], \quad o_2 = \left[O_{2x}, O_{2y}\right].$$

Let the corresponding projected points of a certain point P be u_1 and u_2 respectively. According to (3.7), the displacement between these points will be

$$\boldsymbol{u}_2 - \boldsymbol{u}_1 = -\frac{1}{h}\left(\boldsymbol{o}_2 - \boldsymbol{o}_1\right). \tag{3.10}$$

Thus, the displacement of the projected points is reduced by a factor of h and is either in the opposite or the same direction with respect to the displacement of the viewing points, depending on the sign of h.

3.4   Projection in polar coordinates

Each point in a plane can be defined by a radius vector $\boldsymbol{r}$, which is the vector drawn from the coordinates system origin to the given point. In polar coordinates, a point is defined by the length r of its radius vector and the angle θ that it makes with respect to a given line. If the line is chosen to be the x-axis, the relation between the cartesian coordinates (x,y) and the polar coordinates (r,θ) of a point are

$$r = \sqrt{x^2 + y^2},$$

$$\theta = \tan^{-1}\left(\frac{y}{x}\right).$$

The polar coordinates are defined for the whole plane except the origin, where the angle θ is undefined. The r polar coordinate is the length of the radius vector:

$$r = |\boldsymbol{r}|.$$

Let us consider two parallel vectors $\boldsymbol{a}$, $\boldsymbol{b}$, and their sum

$$\boldsymbol{c} = \boldsymbol{a} + \boldsymbol{b}.$$

This is illustrated in Figure 15. The vector $\boldsymbol{c}$ is drawn with a slight offset with respect to vectors $\boldsymbol{a}$ and $\boldsymbol{b}$ for the sake of clarity. It is easy to show that in such case

$$r_c = r_a + r_b,$$
$$\theta_c = \theta_a = \theta_b. \tag{3.11}$$

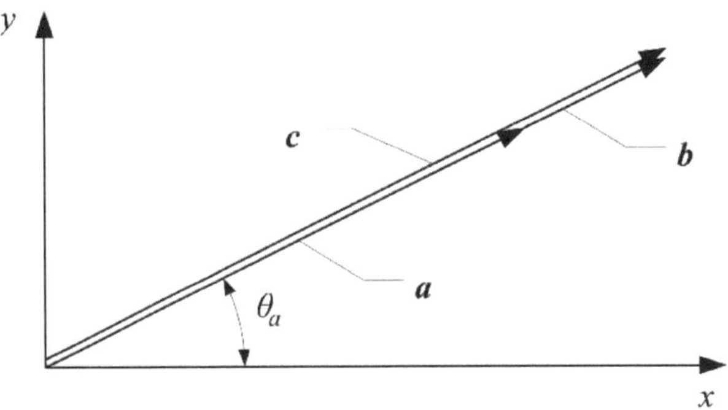

Figure 15: Addition of two parallel vectors

Let us assume that the vectors u and o in (3.8) are parallel. This condition can be written as

$$\theta_u = \theta_o. \tag{3.12}$$

In such a case, according to (3.11)

$$r_x = \frac{r_u}{\alpha_h} + \frac{r_o}{1+h},$$

and

$$\theta_x = \theta_u = \theta_o.$$

Let us modify the vector u in (3.8) by adding to it an infinitesimal vector du, such that

$$du = dr \cdot \hat{r}(\theta),$$

where $\hat{r}(\theta)$ is a unit vector in the direction of u. By definition, the vector du is parallel to u. Again, according to (3.11), such an operation modifies the vector x by

$$dx = \frac{dr}{\alpha(u)} \hat{r}(\theta), \tag{3.13}$$

which can also be written as

$$\frac{dx}{dr} = \frac{\hat{r}(\theta)}{\alpha(u)}. \tag{3.14}$$

4 DISPLAYED IMAGE IN PROJECTED ASSEMBLIES

4.1 Construction of projected assemblies

In our generic description of bulk moiré assemblies (Chapter 2) we defined certain contents for the assembly's planes: a structure for the front plane and an image for the backplane. Projected assemblies contain an additional element: the primitive image.

As explained in sub-Chapter 2.5, the front plane area is divided into an array of identical cells, which are part of the front plane structure. The primitive image is created by defining identical graphics for all these cells. This creates a periodic image with the same basis vectors as the front plane structure. The primitive image is deposited on the front plane and is an important tool for the following analysis.

A projected assembly is created by projecting the front plane objects (its structure and the primitive image) onto the backplane. This projection is accomplished using two different projection points. The center objects are projected using the viewing point as the projection point. All other objects of the front plane, including the primitive image, are projected using another projection point, which will be called the "assembly projection point." The projected primitive image becomes the backplane image in projected assemblies. The distance of the assembly projection point from the front plane will be denoted by H and its normalized value by h (3.3).

According to the discussion in sub-Chapter 3.2, the backplane and the primitive images are related by scaling and shift. Therefore, the backplane image in projected assemblies is also periodic with the same dimensionality as the assembly. The basis vectors of the backplane image are parallel to the basis vectors of the primitive image, but generally have a different magnitude.

The construction of the projected assembly is illustrated in Figure 16. The set of the projected center objects will be called "sampling structure," and it is either a grid or a lattice. Each sampling element of the sampling structure is uniquely associated with a cell of the front plane structure.

4.2 Displayed image forming

The mechanism that forms the displayed image varies for different assemblies. However, all assemblies share certain fundamental characteristics, which allow us to carry out a generic analysis that applies to all.

As we will show, the displayed image of bulk moiré assemblies appears floating in space when viewed with both eyes. This happens because the image is dynamic; it changes with the viewer's position. The perceived location of the displayed image must be distinguished from its optical location, which is in the vicinity of the front plane.

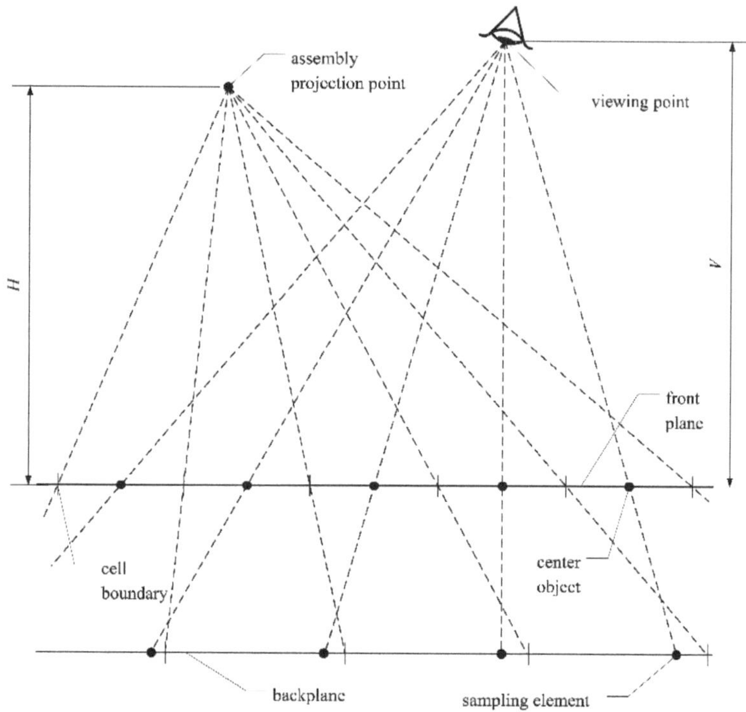

Figure 16:   Backplane objects in the projected assembly

The cells of the front plane structure divide the displayed image also into cells. Two mechanisms form the displayed graphics in each cell:

1.   Sampling: Extraction of graphical information from the backplane image by the corresponding sampling object,

2.   Imaging: The imaging mechanism creates the displayed cell graphics from the sampled graphics.

These mechanisms act simultaneously. They are separated here only conceptually for the sake of simplifying the analysis. The cell image creation process in a 2D assembly is illustrated schematically in Figure 17.

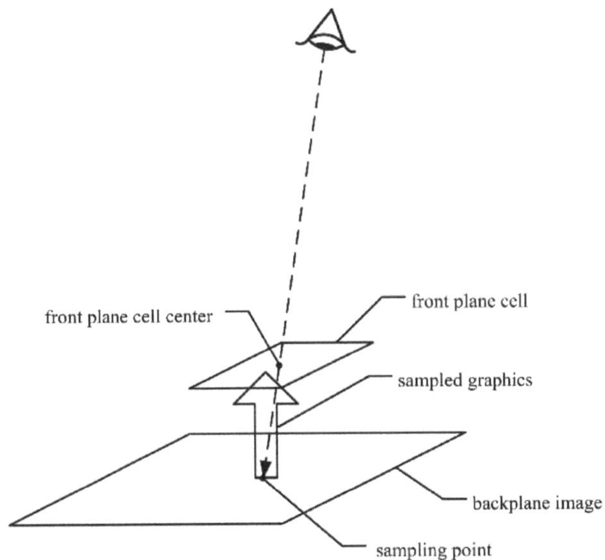

Figure 17: Schematic illustration of the image forming process in a 2D assembly

Sampling depends on the location of the sampling element within the backplane image. Therefore, the same sampling element will yield different sampled graphics in different locations. On the other hand, the imaging mechanism depends only on the sampled graphics and is independent of the location of the sampling object.

Unlike the backplane image, in which all cells have identical graphics, the displayed image cells generally have different graphics. This is because the backplane image and the sampling structure generally have different periods. The displayed image is still periodic, but its period (or periods) is typically much larger than the period (or periods) of the backplane image.

Let us introduce an image creation operator for the k'th cell:

$$\Lambda_k = G_k\{\Phi\}, \tag{4.1}$$

where Φ is the backplane image, and Λ_k is the displayed image of the k'th cell. The operator G_k depends on the location of its corresponding sampling element. The index k denotes a single integer in 1D assemblies and a pair of integers in 2D assemblies. The full displayed image creation operator is the union of all the cell creation operators:

$$G = \bigcup_k G_k,$$

so

$$\Lambda = G\{\Phi\}, \tag{4.2}$$

where Λ is the displayed image.

4.3 Image creation in one-dimensional assemblies

4.3.1 The backplane image

In the present context, we denote the period of the primitive image by p. The backplane image in a 1D projected assembly is a projection of the primitive image from the assembly projection point. This backplane image is one-dimensional with a period

$$p_b = \alpha_h p, \tag{4.3}$$

where the projection constant α_h is given by (3.2).

4.3.2 The sampling grid

In 1D assemblies, the center objects form a grid, so the sampling structure is a grid too. The step of the sampling grid will be

$$p_s = \alpha_v p, \tag{4.4}$$

where α_v is the projection constant (3.2)

$$\alpha_v = 1 + \frac{t}{V} = 1 + \frac{1}{v}, \tag{4.5}$$

V is the distance of the viewing point from the front plane, and

$$v = \frac{V}{t}.$$

is the normalized viewing distance. The sampling grid coordinates are

$$x^s_{\ k} = x^s_{\ 0} + k p_s.$$

4.3.3 Equivalent grids

The image forming operator G (4.2) depends on the coordinates of the sampling gridlines. Let us insert the coordinate parameters in (4.2) to show this dependence explicitly:

$$\Lambda = G\left(x_0, p_s\right)\{\Phi\}. \tag{4.6}$$

The image-forming operator G is not unique; any sampling gridline can be translated by a whole multiple of the assembly image period without affecting the displayed image. The validity of this claim stems from the fact that a sampling gridline translated by a whole multiple of the image period will sample the same graphics as the original gridline, with the image being translated by the same amount but in the opposite direction. But a translation of the image by a whole multiple of its period leaves it intact. Therefore, the translated gridline will sample the same graphics as before the translation. Mathematically, we may state this as follows:

$$\Lambda = G\left(x_0 + np_b, p_s\right)\{\Phi\} \qquad (4.7)$$

for any integer n. Generally, if a certain grid (acting as a sampling grid) creates the same displayed image as the original sampling grid, we will call it an "equivalent grid."

4.3.4   The collapsed grid

The grids in (4.7) are an example of equivalent grids derived from the sampling grid by a uniform translation of the whole grid. Such grids have the same step as the original grid. However, there are also equivalent grids with different step sizes, derived from the sampling grid by shifting its gridlines by different amounts. Such an operation may create non-equidistant grids. However, here we will consider only equidistant equivalent grids. In this set of equivalent grids, there is generally one with the smallest step (in absolute value). We will call this grid "collapsed."

Figure 18 illustrates how a collapsed grid is constructed. Let us consider first the upper part of Figure 18, labeled "Normal." This diagram shows the zeroth and the first sampling gridlines. It also shows an imaginary cell of width p_b (the backplane image period) with the zeroth sampling gridline at its center. There will always be an integer n such that shifting the first sampling gridline by np_b to the left will place it in this imaginary cell. In Figure 18, the sampling gridlines are shown as solid lines, and a dashed line indicates the shifted gridline. The arrows denote the shifting.

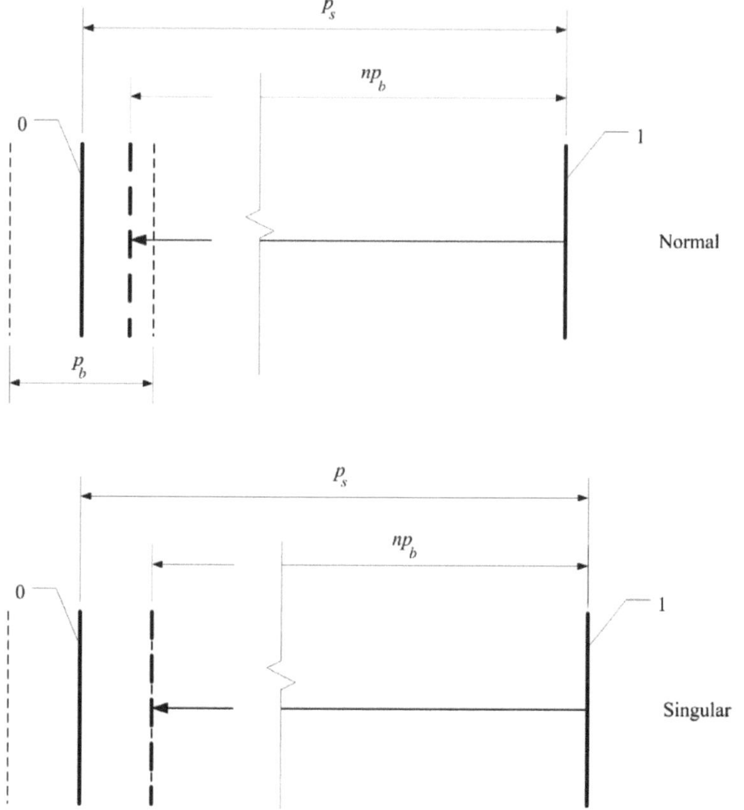

Figure 18: Construction of the collapsed grid

Mathematically, *n* is defined by the inequality

$$\left| p_s - np_b \right| \le \frac{p_b}{2}.$$

(4.8)

In the normal case shown in the upper part of Figure 18, this equation has a single solution. Let us now consider the grid

$$\xi_k = x^s_{\,0} + kp_s - knp_b = x^s_{\,0} + k\left(p_s - np_b \right).$$

(4.9)

The step δ of this grid is

$$\delta = p_s - np_b.$$

The grid (4.9) is equivalent because its gridlines are shifted by an integer multiple of the image period. It is also the equivalent grid with the smallest possible step (in absolute value).

In the singular case shown in Figure 18, there is an integer n such that

$$p_s - np_b = \frac{p_b}{2},$$

$$p_s - (n+1)p_b = -\frac{p_b}{2},$$

so (4.8) has two solutions: n and $n + 1$. These two solutions can be used to define two different equivalent grids, one with a step $p_b/2$ and the other with a step $-p_b/2$. Therefore, in the singular case, the collapsed grid is not unique.

We will encounter situations in which the step of the collapsed grid varies continuously. When the step absolute value is close to $p_b/2$, a small step variation may cause a non-continuous sign change in the collapsed grid. This, in turn, causes undesired visual effects in the displayed image. However, this book will focus on cases where the discrepancy between the sampling grid step and the image period is very small. If this discrepancy is small enough, the occurrence of the said singularity is avoided. It will be helpful to relate the sampling grid step and the image period by

$$p_s = (1+\varepsilon) p_b, \tag{4.10}$$

where ε is the normalized discrepancy between the image and the sampling grid periods. The singularity is avoided if

$$|\varepsilon| < \frac{1}{2}. \tag{4.11}$$

This case is illustrated in Figure 19, in which (4.8) has a unique solution $n = 1$, and the step of the collapsed grid is

$$\delta = p_s - p_b = \varepsilon p_b. \tag{4.12}$$

Given (4.3) and (4.4), the step of the collapsed grid can also be written as

$$\delta = p_s - p_b = \frac{h-v}{hv} p. \tag{4.13}$$

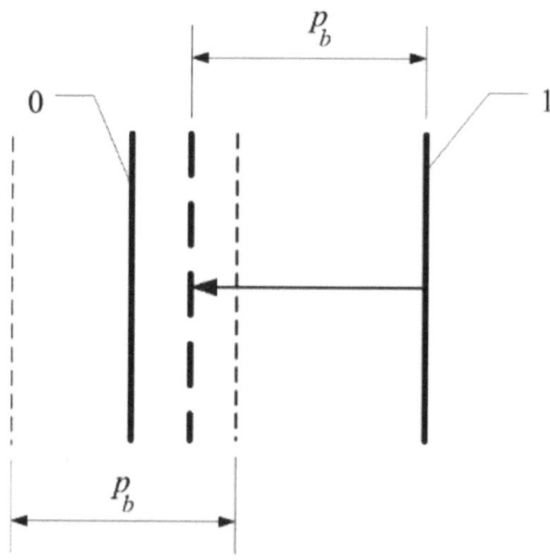

Figure 19:   Grid collapsing for the small discrepancy case

The collapsed grid coordinates are:

$$\xi_k = \xi_0 + k\delta.$$

The origins of the sampling and collapsed grids coincide. However, the step of the collapsed grid is εp_b, which can be much smaller than both the original sampling grid step p_s and the image period p_b. Using the collapsed grid as the sampling structure, (4.6) can be rewritten as

$$\Lambda = G\left(\xi_0, \delta\right)\{\Phi\}.$$

Figure 20 shows a typical collapsed grid superimposed on the backplane image cell, which contains the collapsed grid origin (the line with index $k = 0$). The behavior of the collapsed grid depends on the sign of ε, which can be either positive or negative. When $\varepsilon > 0$, the coordinates of the collapsed grid increase with increasing index. When $\varepsilon < 0$, this behavior is reversed, and the coordinates of the collapsed grid decrease as the index increases. These behaviors are illustrated in Figure 20.

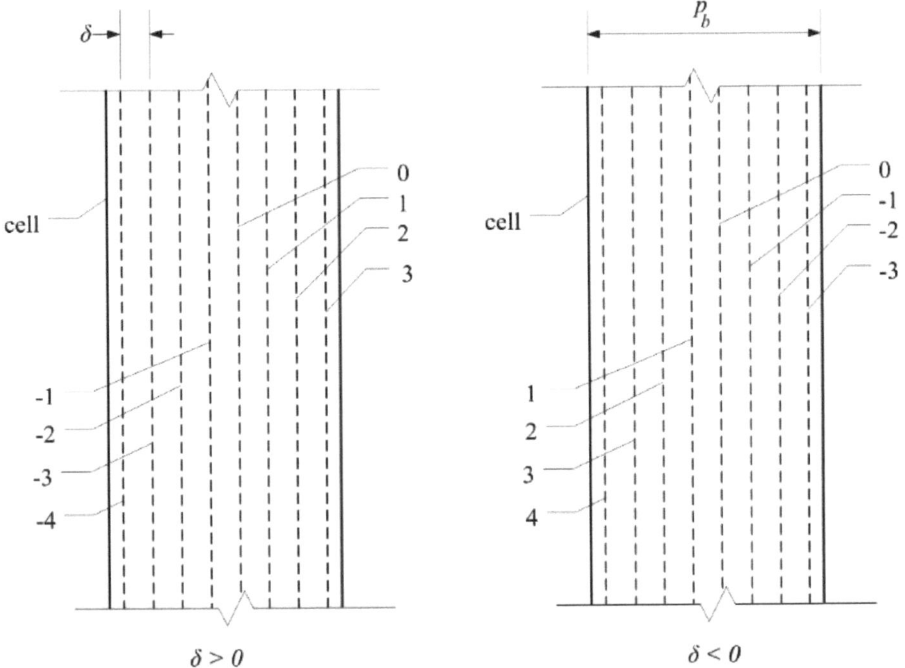

Figure 20:   The collapsed grid superimposed on a backplane image cell

4.3.5   The displayed image

Let us assume that the discrepancy ε is a whole divisor of 1, so that:

$$N = \frac{1}{\varepsilon},\tag{4.14}$$

where N is an integer. In such a case

$$\xi_{k+N} = \xi_k + \varepsilon N p_b = \xi_k + p_b.\tag{4.15}$$

The gridlines ξ_{k+N} and ξ_k are in different locations of the assembly image, but as argued already, shifting a sampling gridline by the image period does not affect the sampled graphics. Therefore, cells k and $k + N$ of the displayed image will contain identical images.

In sub-Chapter 4.2 we used the front plane cells to partition the displayed image. In the 1D assembly, these cells are vertical bands of width p. Therefore, the distance between the displayed image cells k and $k + N$ is Np. Since (4.15) is valid for any k, it follows that the displayed image is periodic too, with a period of Np. Therefore, we can define a magnification for the displayed image as the ratio between the displayed and the backplane image periods:

$$M = \frac{Np}{p_b} = \frac{p}{\delta}.$$

(4.16)

The analysis leading to this definition depends on the assumption that N in (4.14) is an integer. In general, this is not the case. When N is not an integer, the displayed image is periodic only in a certain average sense and displays spatial undulations of the order of p. These effects are hardly noticeable in practice, and we will not treat them. Instead, we will regard the displayed image as being periodic even if N is not an integer and will use (4.16) as a definition of the assembly magnification for any value of N.

We have already noted that the step of the collapsed grid can be either positive or negative, and so can N. Therefore, the magnification is also a signed quantity. The sign of the magnification has a visual impact on the displayed image.

According to (4.13) and (4.16), the magnification of a 1D projected assembly is

$$M = \frac{hv}{h-v}.$$

(4.17)

The distances v and h are signed, and the positive direction is defined in Figure 11. In optical assemblies, v must be positive (these assemblies cannot be viewed from behind). On the other hand, h can be either positive or negative.

The magnification M can also be either positive or negative, depending on the values of v and h. In many cases $|V| \gg |H|$. In such cases, it is possible to approximate

$$M \approx -h,$$

(4.18)

and the magnification becomes independent of the viewing distance. Note that this magnification is negative for protruding objects (characterized by $h > 0$).

4.4   Image creation in two-dimensional assemblies

4.4.1   The backplane image

We noted already in sub-Chapter 4.1 that the primitive image basis vectors are identical to the front structure basis vectors. Let us denote these basis vectors by p and q. In 2D assemblies, the backplane image is periodic in two dimensions, and its basis vectors are mutually parallel to p and q:

$$p_b = \alpha_h p, \quad q_b = \alpha_h q,$$

(4.19)

where α_h is the projection constant corresponding to the assembly projection point.

4.4.2   The sampling lattice

In 2D assemblies, the sampling structure is a lattice, which is a projection of the front plane center objects lattice. The front structure basis vectors p and q are also the basis vectors of the center objects lattice. We can use (2.4) and (3.7) to derive the coordinates of the sampling lattice points:

$$x^s{}_{k,l} = \alpha_v \left(x_{0,0} + S_{k,l} \right) - \frac{o}{v}, \tag{4.20}$$

where o is the footprint of the viewing point on the front plane. The coordinates of the sampling lattice can also be written as

$$x^s{}_{k,l} = x^s{}_{0,0} + k p_s + l q_s, \tag{4.21}$$

where the basis vectors of the sampling lattice are given by

$$p_s = \alpha_v p, \quad q_s = \alpha_v q, \tag{4.22}$$

and the lattice origin by

$$x^s{}_{0,0} = \alpha_v x_{0,0} - \frac{o}{v}. \tag{4.23}$$

4.4.3   Equivalent lattices

Analogously to the one-dimensional case discussed in sub-Chapter 4.3.3, if a certain lattice creates the same displayed image as the sampling lattice, we will call it an "equivalent lattice." Let F be the image-forming operator in 2D assemblies:

$$\Lambda = F\left(x^s{}_{0,0}, p_s, q_s \right)\{\Phi\}. \tag{4.23}$$

This operator depends on the lattice origin and its basis vectors. A shift of the sampling lattice by a back image vector (2.3) does not affect the displayed image:

$$\Lambda = F\left(x^s{}_{0,0} + P_{k,l}, p_s, q_s \right)\{\Phi\}. \tag{4.24}$$

Therefore, the lattices in (4.24) are equivalent lattices for all integers k and l.

4.4.4   The collapsed lattice

Equivalent lattices can have basis vectors with different magnitudes. In analogy to sub-Chapter 4.3.4, we define the collapsed lattice as the equivalent lattice with basis vectors having the smallest basis vectors magnitudes.

Here too, it is convenient to introduce normalized discrepancies ε and η:

$$p_s = \left(1+\varepsilon\right) p_b, \quad q_s = \left(1+\eta\right) q_b. \tag{4.25}$$

In analogy to (4.8), let us consider the inequalities

$$\left| \boldsymbol{p}_s - n\boldsymbol{p}_b \right| \le \frac{\left| \boldsymbol{p}_b \right|}{2},$$
(4.26)

and

$$\left| \boldsymbol{q}_s - m\boldsymbol{q}_b \right| \le \frac{\left| \boldsymbol{q}_b \right|}{2}.$$
(4.27)

Again, in certain singular cases, (4.26) or (4.27) may have two solutions. But also in the two-dimensional case, our analysis will be limited to small discrepancy cases in which

$$\left| \varepsilon \right|, \ \left| \eta \right| \ll 1$$

In such cases, the solution to (4.26) and (4.27) is $n = m = 1$, and the collapsed lattice vectors become

$$\boldsymbol{\delta} = \boldsymbol{p}_s - \boldsymbol{p}_b = \varepsilon \boldsymbol{p}_b, \quad \boldsymbol{\gamma} = \boldsymbol{q}_s - \boldsymbol{q}_b = \eta \boldsymbol{q}_b,$$
(4.28)

and, in a different form

$$\boldsymbol{\delta} = \boldsymbol{p}_s - \boldsymbol{p}_b = \frac{h-v}{hv}\boldsymbol{p}, \quad \boldsymbol{\gamma} = \boldsymbol{q}_s - \boldsymbol{q}_b = \frac{h-v}{hv}\boldsymbol{q}.$$
(4.29)

Correspondingly, the collapsed lattice coordinates are

$$\boldsymbol{\xi}_{n,m} = \boldsymbol{\xi}_{0,0} + n\boldsymbol{\delta} + m\boldsymbol{\gamma}.$$

The displayed image can be represented as

$$\Lambda = F\left(\boldsymbol{\xi}_{0,0}, \boldsymbol{\delta}, \boldsymbol{\gamma} \right)\{\Phi\}.$$

For example, consider the square lattice. In this case, the image cells are squares. This case is illustrated in Figure 21, which shows that collapsed grid points superimposed on the backplane image cell, which contains the collapsed grid origin. In this example $\varepsilon = \eta$, and $\varepsilon > 0$. The indices of the origin and its immediate neighbors are also shown.

4.4.5 The displayed image magnification

Let us assume that the normalized discrepancies ε and η are whole divisors of 1, so their inverses are integers:

$$K = \frac{1}{\varepsilon}, \quad L = \frac{1}{\eta},$$
(4.30)

where K and L are (signed) integers. Let us consider the lattice point $\xi_{n+K,m}$:

$$\xi_{n+K,m} = \xi_{n,m} + K\varepsilon\,\boldsymbol{p}_b = \xi_{n,m} + \boldsymbol{p}_b. \qquad (4.31)$$

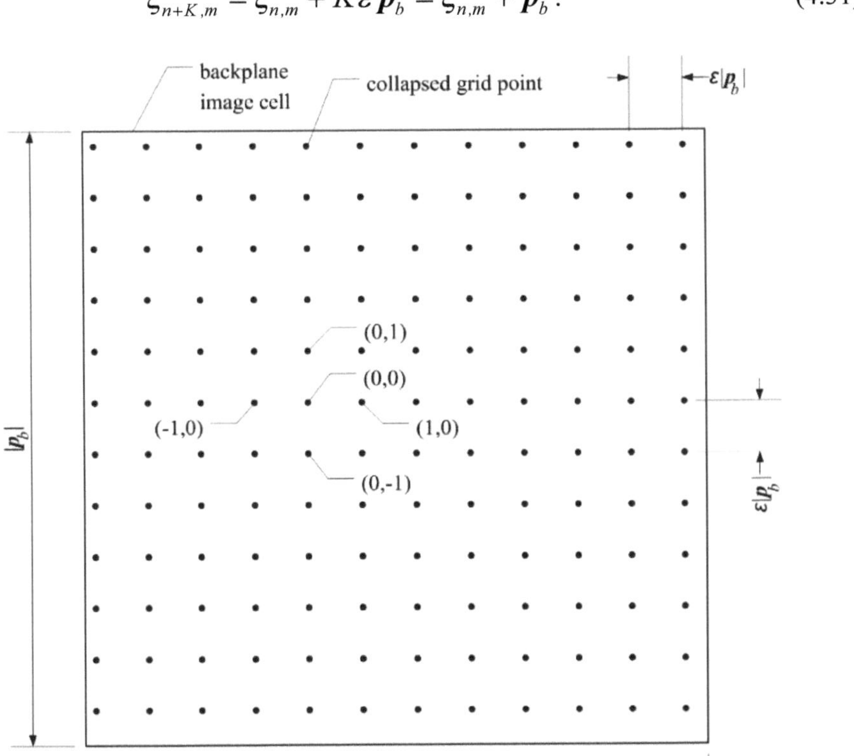

Figure 21:   The collapsed grid for a square lattice with $\varepsilon > 0$

The lattice points $\xi_{n+K,m}$ and $\xi_{n,m}$ are shifted one with respect to the other by an image vector so that they will produce identical sampled graphics, and their corresponding cells of the displayed image will be identical. Similarly,

$$\xi_{n,m+L} = \xi_{n,m} + L\eta\,\boldsymbol{q}_b = \xi_{n,m} + \boldsymbol{q}_b, \qquad (4.32)$$

and again, cells $(n, m+L)$ and (n, m) in the displayed image will be identical. Since (4.31) and (4.32) are valid for all pairs of indices (n, m), the displayed image has a dimensionality of 2 with basis vectors $K\boldsymbol{p}$ and $L\boldsymbol{q}$. In complete analogy to the one-dimensional case, we can introduce the magnification M for the displayed image:

$$M = \frac{|p|}{|\delta|} = \frac{|q|}{|\gamma|} = \frac{hv}{h-v},$$

which is identical to the magnification of the 1D assembly (4.17).

5 THE 3D ILLUSION MECHANISM

When an observer looks at an object, each eye projects it onto the corresponding retina. Since the eyes are at different points in space, their retinal projections differ. These differences are analyzed by the human brain, which creates a 3D sensation.

Suppose that the observer's eyes were exposed to two images, each showing a different projection of an object. Such images are called a "stereo pair" (Stereoscopy, 2022). When a stereo pair is observed with a stereo-viewing device (Sterescope, 2023), the eyes create projections on the on the retina from these images. The human brain cannot discern a real projection from a projection of a projection. Therefore, such exposure may artificially invoke a 3D sensation. This principle is used in stereo-viewing devices.

Let us consider a certain reference plane, a point object in space, and an observer free to move on a plane parallel to the reference plane. Let us assume that the observer makes a certain movement, which will be denoted by E. This scenario is illustrated in Figure 22 and Figure 23.

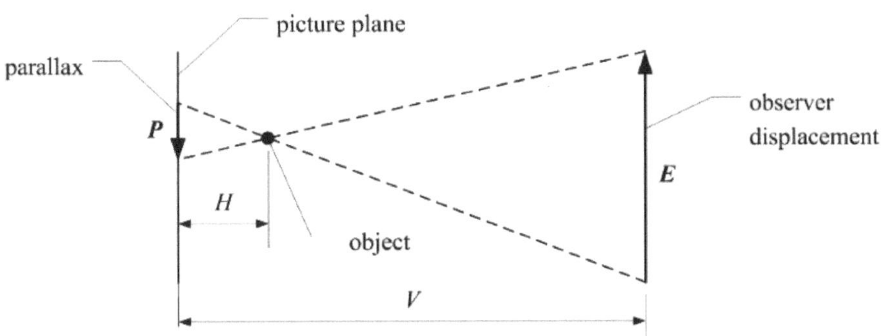

Figure 22: The parallax of a point object in front of a plane

Let us now consider the projection of the object point on the reference plane, using one of the observer's eyes as the projection point. When the observer moves, the projection of the point object on the reference plane moves too. For a given observer displacement E, there is a certain displacement P of the projected point object on the reference plane. This displacement is called parallax, a key concept in understanding 3D illusions.

From Figure 22 and Figure 23, it is evident that the parallax vector is either parallel or anti-parallel to the displacement vector, depending on whether the object point is in front or behind the reference plane, respectively. The relation between the lengths of these vectors can be derived from known geometrical theorems concerning triangles similarity.

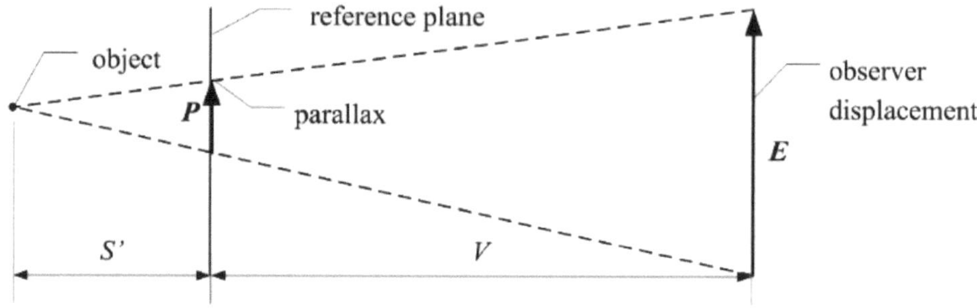

Figure 23: The parallax of a point object behind a plane

Let us consider Figure 22. From triangles similarity, it follows that

$$P = -\frac{H}{V-H}E,$$

(5.1)

where the minus sign on the right-hand side was inserted because, in this case, the parallax was anti-parallel to the displacement. Let us now consider Figure 23. In this case

$$P = \frac{S'}{V+S'}E.$$

(5.2)

Equations (5.1) and (5.2) can be unified if we let H be a signed quantity. Let the distance be negative if the point to which it corresponds lies behind the picture plane, and positive otherwise. Equation (5.2) was derived by treating S' as positive. Let S be the signed distance, and according to our convention, it is negative in this case, so $S' = -S$. Expressing (5.2) in terms of S, we get

$$P = -\frac{S}{V-S}E,$$

(5.3)

which is identical to (5.1) except for replacing H with S. Thus, with our sign convention (5.1) is valid for objects both in front and behind the reference surface.

Let us now consider a system that can display an image on a particular screen that moves in response to the observer's movement. If, for a given observer movement (on a plane parallel to the reference plane), all points of the displayed image are shifted by the same parallax, and this parallax is related to the observer's displacement by (5.1), the image will be conceived as appearing on a plane at a distance H from the system's reference plane.

Let us further consider the human viewing scenario shown in Figure 24. In the top part, we show an imaginary scenario in which the observer's right eye is superimposed on their left eye. Their right eye is moved to its natural position at the bottom. This movement causes the image to shift by a parallax vector $\boldsymbol{P}$. The left eye, however, remained stationary, and its displayed image did not change. As a result, the observer's two eyes are exposed to a pair of images that are shifted one with respect to the other. We assume that the observer's head is upright. In this case, the vector $\boldsymbol{E}$ (5.1) is the ocular vector $\boldsymbol{e}$. The corresponding parallax is called "visual" and is denoted by $\boldsymbol{P}_V$:

$$\boldsymbol{P}_V = \frac{H}{H-V}\boldsymbol{e} \,. \tag{5.4}$$

Now, assume that the viewer is exposed to a particular system with 3D illusion capability instead of the point object. Such a system can display a different image for each of the observer's eyes, as shown in Figure 25. When the views are superimposed, the points exhibit a parallax P. The observer cannot discern the view of the real object, as shown in Figure 24, from the views they perceive with their eyes when exposed to the 3D illusion. If the displayed parallax equals the visual parallax (5.4), the observer will perceive an object floating in space at a distance H from the screen.

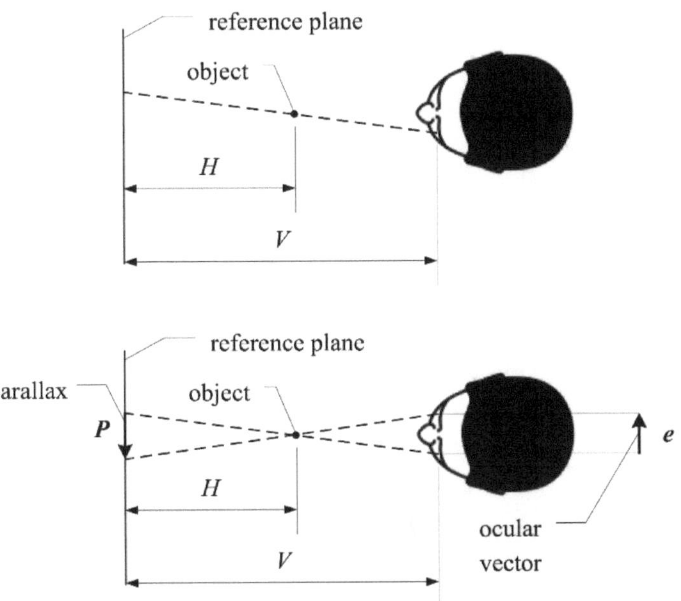

Figure 24: Visual parallax. Top: right eye superimposed in the left eye, bottom: right eye moved to its natural position

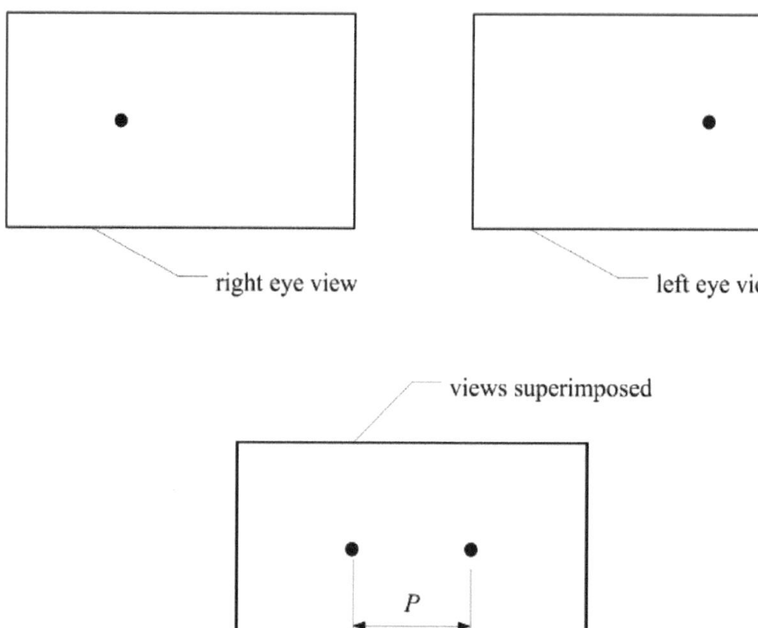

Figure 25:   3D illusion system views

6 3D CHARACTERISTICS OF THE DISPLAYED IMAGE IN PROJECTED ASSEMBLIES

6.1   3D characteristics of one-dimensional projected assemblies

6.1.1   Displacement of the sampling grid

Since the observation point serves as the sampling grid's projection center, its movement causes the grid to move.

Let us consider a displacement f of the viewing point in a plane parallel to the front plane and by σ the corresponding displacement of the sampling grid. We adopt the two-dimensional notation for f and σ by dropping the z coordinates (see sub-Chapter 3.2). According to (3.10)

$$\sigma = -\frac{f}{v}.\qquad(6.1)$$

The y component of σ displaces the gridlines along their direction and does not affect the position of the sampling grid. The shifted sampling grid coordinates are given by

$$x'^{s}_{k} = \sigma_x + x^{s}_0 + kp_s.\qquad(6.2)$$

6.1.2   Displacement of the displayed image

Let us denote the collapsed grid step by δ and assume that it is a whole divisor of σ_x, namely, that there is an integer N such that

$$N = \frac{\sigma_x}{\delta}.\qquad(6.3)$$

In such cases,

$$\xi_{k+N} = \xi_k + \sigma_x.$$

Let us consider an arbitrary front plane cell k. This cell is associated with a collapsed gridline with the coordinate ξ_k. The graphics displayed by this cell is $G_k\left(\xi_k\right)\{\Phi\}$. Cells k and $k+N$ display images sampled from the background image at a distance of σ_x apart. Since the cell width of the front plane structure is p, these images will be displayed by a space Np apart:

$$Np = \frac{\sigma_x}{\delta}p = M\sigma_x.\qquad(6.4)$$

Equation (6.4) demonstrates the significance of the moiré magnification: graphics sampled at a certain distance σ_x apart will be displayed at this distance multiplied by the moiré magnification. This is illustrated in Figure 26.

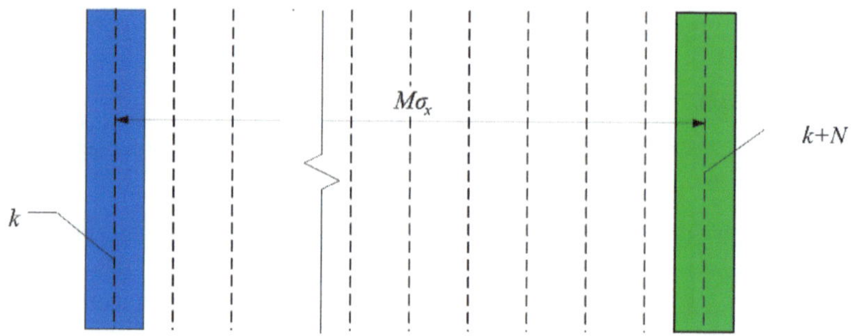

Figure 26:   Displayed graphics in cells k and N before movement

The same scenario after the viewing point movement is shown in Figure 27.

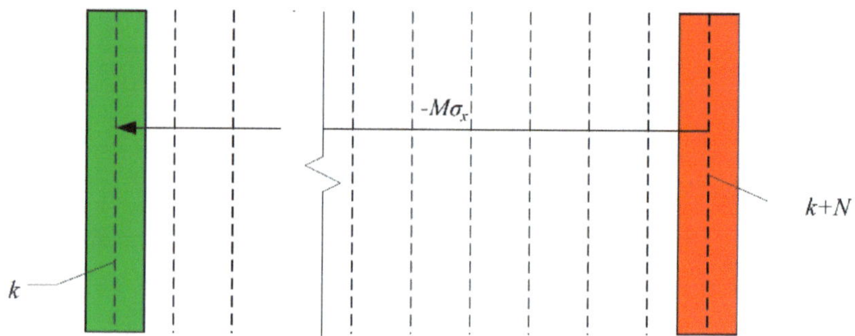

Figure 27:   Displayed graphics after the viewing point movement

The collapsed gridline of cell k is now at $\xi_k + \sigma_x$, so the image displayed by cell k will be $G_k\left(\xi_A + \sigma_x\right)\{\Phi\}$. This image was displayed before the movement in lenticule $k+N$. We may say that the graphics displayed by cell $k+N$ is displaced by $-M\sigma_x$. Since this is true for all k, we may conclude that the whole displayed image is shifted by $-M\sigma_x$.

If N is not an integer, the displayed image displacement may be non-uniform, exhibiting local undulations of magnitude p. However, in most practical scenarios, this effect will be hardly noticeable and will not be treated here.

Using (6.1), we can now express the displayed image displacement in terms of the observer displacement:

$$D = \frac{M}{v} f_x .$$

(6.5)

If v is positive, (6.5) implies that the displayed image displacement is parallel to the observer's movement x-component for $M > 0$ and anti-parallel otherwise. The movement of the displayed image is confined to the x-direction.

6.1.3   The ambiguity in the displacement magnitude

We have shown that the motion of the viewing point causes a motion of the displayed image. If one could monitor the motion of the displayed image as the viewing point continuously moved, one could have measured the displacement of the displayed image unambiguously. However, if one has only two snapshots of the displayed image, one before the movement and one after it, the displacement between these two snapshots may be different from the actual displacement because the displayed image is periodic in the x direction, with a period of

$$p_d = Mp_b .$$

In other words, all displayed image displacements

$$d_k = d + kp_d$$

will produce the same pair of snapshots for any integer k. The observer's eyes are exposed to snapshots; therefore, the visual displacement may be smaller than the actual displacement.

To deal with this ambiguity, it is helpful to introduce the reduced displacement d_r, which is derived from the true displacement d as follows:

$$d_r = d + kp_d$$

(6.6)

where k is an integer such that

$$|d_r| < \frac{p_d}{2}$$

(6.7)

and

$$sgn(d_r) = sgn(d) .$$

(6.8)

The reduced displacement is shown in Figure 28 as a function of the actual displacement. It is seen that the reduced displacement lies in the interval $\left[-p_d/2, p_d/2\right]$.

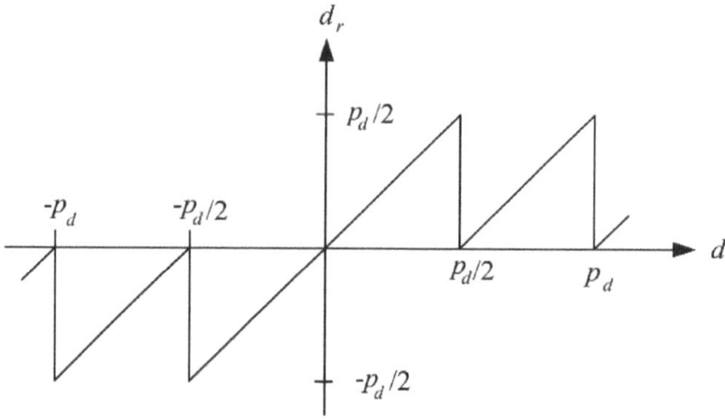

Figure 28: The reduced displacement

An observer will sense the reduced displacement rather than the actual displacement.

6.1.4   The depth of the displayed image

In Chapter 15 we explained the 3D illusion mechanism and noted that it arises when the displayed image moves parallel (or antiparallel) to the observer's motion. The displayed image in the present case exhibits precisely this behavior and, therefore, appears on a plane different from the assembly plane.

Let us consider the movement of the displayed image corresponding to a movement by an ocular vector e. Using (6.1) and (6.5), we get

$$D = \frac{h}{h-v}e_x,\qquad(6.9)$$

where e_x is the x component of e. However, the viewer sees the two images as snapshots of the displayed image and therefore perceives the reduced displacement (6.6) instead of the total displacement. Let us assume for a moment that

$$|D| < p_d.\qquad(6.10)$$

In this case, the true displacement equals its reduced (perceived) value. The displayed image displacement in a vector form is

$$\boldsymbol{D} = \begin{bmatrix} D, & 0 \end{bmatrix}.$$

From (5.4) and (6.9) it is seen that

$$\boldsymbol{P}_V = \boldsymbol{D} \quad \text{when} \quad e = \begin{bmatrix} e_x, 0 \end{bmatrix},\qquad(6.11)$$

or, in other words, the displayed image displacement equals the visual parallax when the observer's ocular vector is in the x direction. In such a case, the displayed image will appear at a distance H from the picture plane. This conclusion does not depend on the observer's location. Therefore, the displayed image will appear on the same plane for all viewing positions.

Let us reconsider the 3D moiré law, which was presented in sub-Chapter 1.4. The primitive image is the front mask, and the shadow shown in Figure 6 is its projection on the backplane. The assembly projection point is the light source. According to the present analysis, the displayed image will appear on a plane passing through the light source and parallel to the assembly, as stated in the law.

6.1.5 Conditions for 3D display fidelity

The correct 3D appearance of the displayed image depends on whether the condition (6.10) is satisfied. This condition can also be written as

$$\left|\frac{h}{h-v}\right| e_x \leq \left|\frac{hv}{h-v}\right| p_b,$$

or

$$e_x \leq vp_b = v\alpha_h p.$$

This sets a constraint on the viewing distance V:

$$V \geq \frac{te_x}{\alpha_h p}. \tag{6.12}$$

In standard lenticular lenses and typical scenarios, $t \approx p$ and $\alpha_h \approx 1$. Therefore, the condition (6.12) can be stated as

$$V \geq\sim e_x. \tag{6.13}$$

The minimal observation distance is limited by the eye's focusing capability, which is about 300mm for most humans. Since typically $|e| \sim 63$mm, the condition (6.13) will be satisfied for all practical viewing scenarios, meaning the perceived displacement will equal its reduced value.

In our discussion of collapsed grids in sub-Chapter 4.3.4, we noted a certain singularity that should be avoided. This singularity arises when the absolute value of the normalized discrepancy between the sampling grid step and the image period (4.10) is less than ½ (4.11). From (4.3) and (4.4) it follows that

$$p_s = \frac{\alpha_v}{\alpha_h} p_b,$$

so, the normalized discrepancy in this case is

$$\varepsilon = \frac{\alpha_v - \alpha_h}{\alpha_h} = \frac{h-v}{v(1+h)}.$$

In the lenticular assembly, $v > 0$. The object must be placed before the viewer, not behind them for proper viewing. Therefore, we may assume that $h < v$. Let us consider first the case $h > 0$. In this case $|h - v| = v - h$, so the condition (4.11) takes the form

$$\frac{v-h}{hv} < \frac{1}{2},$$

which can be transformed to

$$h > \frac{2v}{v+2}. \tag{6.14}$$

Let us now consider the case $h < 0$. In this case, the condition (4.11) takes the form

$$\left|\frac{h-v}{hv}\right| = \frac{|h|+v}{|h|v} < \frac{1}{2},$$

which can be transformed to

$$|h| > \frac{2v}{v-2}. \tag{6.15}$$

In many scenarios $v \gg 1$. In such cases the conditions (6.14) and (6.15) can be approximated by

$$|h| > 2. \tag{6.16}$$

This defines a certain neighborhood of the front plane, which is forbidden for the 3D moiré surface (Figure 48).

6.1.6 Generalization of transformations in one-dimensional projected assemblies

In projected assemblies, the backplane image is a projection of the primitive image. This defines a transformation of the primitive image in both the x- and y-directions. However, the position of the moiré surface is determined by the collapsed grid step, as explained in sub-Chapter 6.1.2. This step is determined by the period of the backplane image (4.12), which, in turn, is determined by the x component of the sculpting transformation. The y component of this transformation has no effect on the backplane image period, and therefore also no effect on the moiré surface position. Any transformation of the primitive image in the y-direction will affect the displayed image texture but not its position in space.

In most cases, the absolute value of the normalized height will be much larger than 1. In such cases, the value of the projection constant α_h of the primitive image will be very close to 1. As a result, the projection transformation in the y direction is usually hardly visible, and, in practice, can be neglected. Discarding the transformation in the y direction, (3.7) simplifies to

$$p'_x = \alpha_h p_x - \frac{o_x}{h},$$
$$p'_y = p_y.$$

In some applications, defining a certain transformation in the y-direction may be desirable. Such a transformation can be utilized without affecting the 3D characteristics of the displayed image. So, one can use the following transformation in projected 1D assemblies:

$$p'_x = \alpha_h p_x - \frac{o_x}{h},$$
$$p'_y = f\left(p_y\right).$$

where f is an arbitrary function.

6.2   3D characteristics in two-dimensional projected assemblies

6.2.1   Displacement of the displayed image due to observer movement

The calculation of the displacement of the displayed image due to a movement of the observation point is derived analogously to that for the 1D assemblies.

Let us assume that the motion of the viewing point caused a displacement σ of the sampling lattice, where σ is a collapsed lattice basis vector. This means that for any collapsed lattice point ξ_A, the point

$$\xi_B = \xi_A + \sigma$$

is also a collapsed lattice point. Due to the moiré magnification, the displayed image cells A and B corresponding to the collapsed lattice points ξ_A and ξ_B are displaced by $M\sigma$, as illustrated in Figure 29. The graphics displayed in these cells is shown schematically by hatched textures, and the graphics in the other cells are ignored.

After the displacement, the collapsed grid point of cell A moves to ξ_B, so cell A will display the graphics displayed in cell B before the displacement. The graphics in cell B will also change to other graphics. It will appear to the viewer as if the graphics of cell B was displaced by a vector $-M\sigma$. This is illustrated in Figure 30.

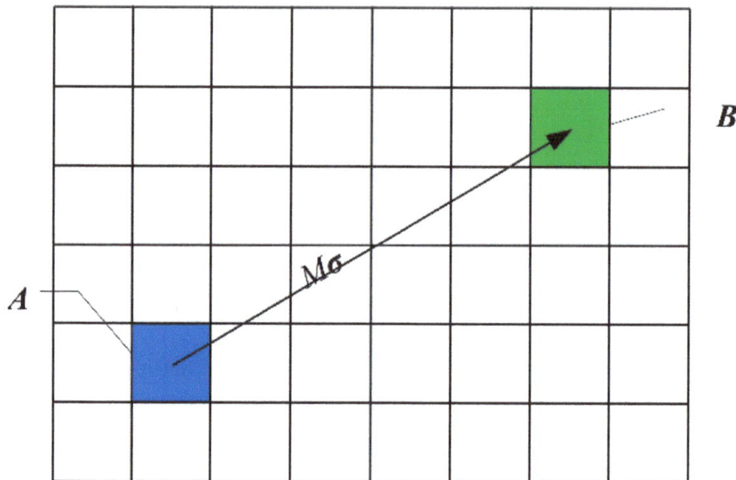

*Figure 29: Cells **A** and **B** before the viewing point displacement*

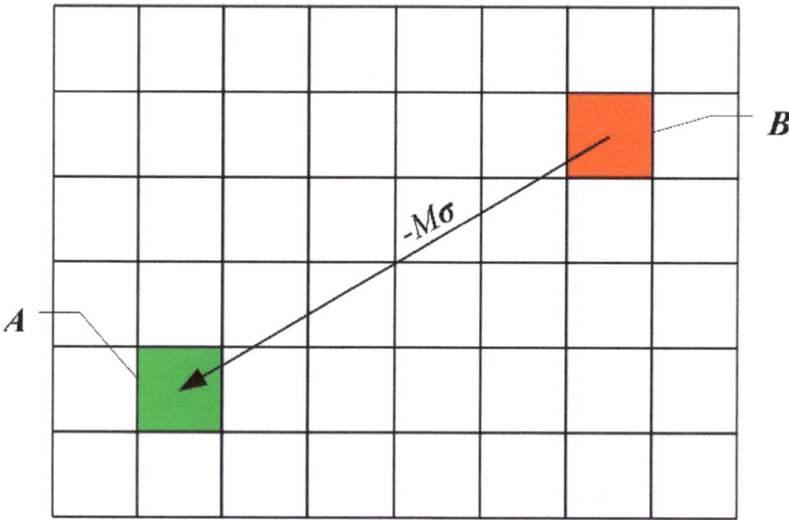

*Figure 30: Cells **A** and **B** after the viewing point displacement*

This argument is valid for any cell of the displayed image. Therefore, the whole displayed image will be displaced by:

$$D = -M\sigma .$$

(6.17)

Given (6.1)

$$D = \frac{M}{v} f .$$ (6.18)

This is the generalization of (6.5) to the 2D case. However, unlike the 1D case, here the image displacement is parallel to the viewer's displacement, generating a two-dimensional parallax. Consequently, the displayed image will exhibit a 3D illusion from all viewer orientations relative to the picture.

Our derivation of the displayed image displacement assumes that the collapsed lattice was displaced by a collapsed grid vector. For general values of lattice movement, the displayed image displacement may be non-uniform and show local undulations with a magnitude of $|p|$ or $|q|$. However, in most practical scenarios, this effect will be hardly noticeable and will not be treated here.

6.2.2   The depth of the displayed image

The calculation of the depth of the displayed image proceeds as in 6.1.4. In the 2D assembly case, Equation (6.9) is replaced by its vector form:

$$D = \frac{h}{h-v} e .$$ (6.19)

The pattern displacement equation (6.19) for ocular movement now becomes identical to the visual parallax equation (5.4). This means that a projected 2D moiré assembly with a projection point at height H and viewed from a distance V will display an image on a plane at a distance H from the assembly. This is the same conclusion as in the 1D case. However, in the 2D case, the ocular vector can have an arbitrary direction, unlike the 1D case, where it had to be perpendicular to the sampling grid direction.

The ocular vector must be parallel to the front plane in both cases.

6.3   Two-dimensional assembly converted to a one-dimensional assembly

Converting the structure of a 2D assembly into a 1D structure can transform it (approximately) into a 1D assembly. However, this conversion has little practical value, as it results in lower visual quality than a native 1D assembly with the same primitive image. Nevertheless, we will discuss this operation here briefly for the sake of completeness.

Imagine a square-shaped structure, like the one depicted in Figure 10. By vertically merging cell columns, one can convert the square cells into vertical bands, akin to a 1D assembly. However, the center object of the converted cell is now a vertical array of points instead of a line, as in the 1D assembly case. This may cause changes in the displayed image in response to a movement in the y direction. This is what we meant when we said above that the conversion is approximate. However, let us ignore this for a moment and proceed to consider another aspect of this conversion.

The primitive image must contain identical graphics in all its cells. The original primitive image satisfies this requirement with respect to the converted structure. If the original primitive image is retained in the converted assembly, the displayed image will remain the same, and the whole operation will be reduced to a formal manipulation of virtual objects. However, once the cell is a vertical band, one can use different graphics for different original cells in the same band, like the graphics shown in Figure 66 below. With such graphics, the displayed image will exhibit 3D characteristics of 1D assemblies; in particular, the 3D effect will be limited to cases where the ocular vector is parallel to the x-direction.

7 SCULPTING OF THE MOIRÉ SURFACE

7.1 The sculpting transformation

In the projected assemblies discussed in Chapter 4, the backplane image was derived by applying a projection transformation to the primitive image. For sculpting, a more general transformation is needed. We call this "sculpting transformation." The sculpted 3D moiré surface has two properties: surface geometry and texture. The surface is specified by the user, and the texture is a mapping of the primitive image on this surface.

There are several methods for mapping an image onto a 3D surface (Texture mapping, 2023), each one leading to a different result. So, for a given surface geometry and primitive image, there may be different 3D moiré surfaces depending on the texture mapping method used. The method proposed here produces visually pleasing results, but we cannot determine to which of the commonly used texture-mapping categories it belongs. The study and the evaluation of other methods in the present context are beyond the scope of this book.

In 3D modeling programs, texture mapping methods are typically designed for continuous surfaces. However, it's important to ensure that the sculpting transformation remains continuous even for non-continuous surfaces to prevent visual distortions and tearing at surface discontinuities. To address this, we have developed a method for deriving continuous sculpting transformations for non-continuous surfaces.

In common nomenclature, a transformation is a function that pairs a transformed point u to a given point x, as in (3.7). We will use the inverse transformation to compute warped images. The inverse transformation gives the original point x for a given transformed coordinate u, like in (3.8). For simplicity, we will call it just "transformation."

7.2 Sculpting transformation continuity

To develop the idea of continuous sculpting transformations, let us consider the surface shown in Figure 31. It is invariant with respect to translation parallel to the v-axis and consists of three planar regions, 1, 2, and 3, with two different heights H_1 and H_2. The backplane coordinates u and v are also shown in Figure 31. The coordinates of the primitive image will be denoted by xy.

The backplane image for the surface shown in Figure 31 can be derived using the ideas outlined in 1.5. Instead of using the same projection point for the whole primitive image, we can use two different points at heights H_1 and H_2. The first point will be used to derive the backplane image in regions 1 and 3, and the second for region 2.

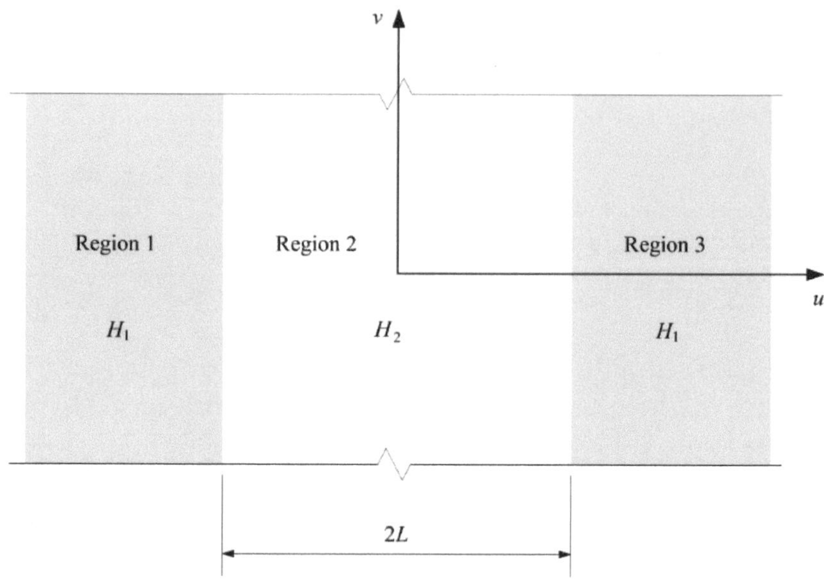

Figure 31: A simple surface

Let us denote the normalized heights of the three different regions by h_1, h_2 and h_3 with $h_3 = h_1$. Correspondingly, we denote the projection constants by α_1, α_2, and α_3 with $\alpha_3 = \alpha_1$. The inverse projection transformations (3.8) for the three regions in Figure 31 are

$$x_k(\boldsymbol{u}) = \frac{\boldsymbol{u}}{\alpha_k} + \frac{\boldsymbol{o}_k}{1+h_k}, \qquad k = 1,2,3 . \tag{7.1}$$

Let us introduce a function $k(\boldsymbol{u})$ which gives the region number to which $\boldsymbol{u}$ belongs. This function can have only three values: 1, 2, and 3. Using this function, we can re-write (7.1) as follows:

$$\boldsymbol{x}(\boldsymbol{u}) = \frac{\boldsymbol{u}}{\alpha_{k(\boldsymbol{u})}} + \frac{\boldsymbol{o}_{k(\boldsymbol{u})}}{1+h_{k(\boldsymbol{u})}} . \tag{7.2}$$

Since the boundaries of the three regions in Figure 31 are vertical lines, we can replace $k(\boldsymbol{u})$ in (7.2) by $k(u)$. Furthermore, as discussed in sub-Chapter 6.1.6, in 1D assemblies, we need only the x-component of the sculpting transformation. In other words, we will deal only with the x-component of (7.2):

$$x(u) = \frac{u}{\alpha_{k(u)}} + \frac{o^x{}_{k(u)}}{1 + h_{k(u)}}.$$

These projection transformations contain three undetermined constants $o^x{}_k$. Let us see what happens if we set these constants to 0. Denoting the resulting transformation by $x_0(u)$, we get

$$x_0(u) = \begin{cases} \dfrac{u}{\alpha_1} & \text{for } |u| \le L \\[2ex] \dfrac{u}{\alpha_2} & \text{for } |u| > L \end{cases} \qquad (7.3)$$

For the sake of the example, let us assume that $h_1 < h_2$, so $\alpha_1 > \alpha_2$. The function $x_0(u)$ is shown schematically in Figure 32. This function exhibits discontinuities at points -L and L.

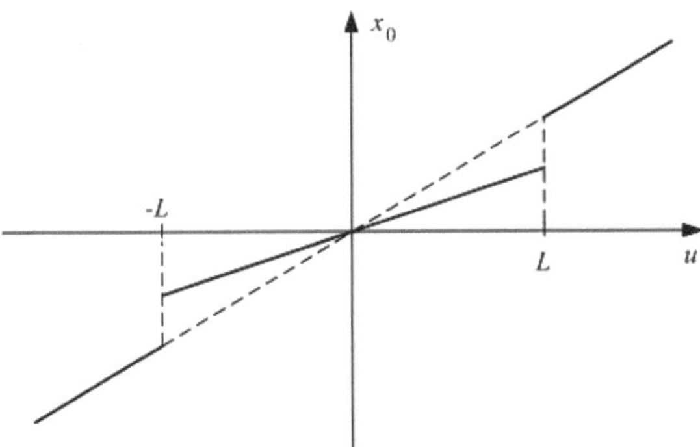

Figure 32:   The non-continuous sculpting transformation

To avoid this discontinuity, we can define the constants $o^x{}_k$ as follows:

$$o^x{}_k = \begin{cases} -\dfrac{L(\alpha_2 - \alpha_1)}{\alpha_1\alpha_2} & \text{for } k = 1 \\[2ex] 0 & \text{for } k = 2 \\[2ex] \dfrac{L(\alpha_2 - \alpha_1)}{\alpha_1\alpha_2} & \text{for } k = 3 \end{cases},$$

in which case the sculpting transformation takes the form:

$$x(u) = \begin{cases} \dfrac{u}{\alpha_2} - \dfrac{L(\alpha_2 - \alpha_1)}{\alpha_1\alpha_2} & \text{for } u < -L \\[2ex] \dfrac{u}{\alpha_1} & \text{for } |u| \le L \\[2ex] \dfrac{u}{\alpha_2} + \dfrac{L(\alpha_2 - \alpha_1)}{\alpha_1\alpha_2} & \text{for } u > L \end{cases}. \tag{7.4}$$

This function is now continuous, as shown in Figure 33.

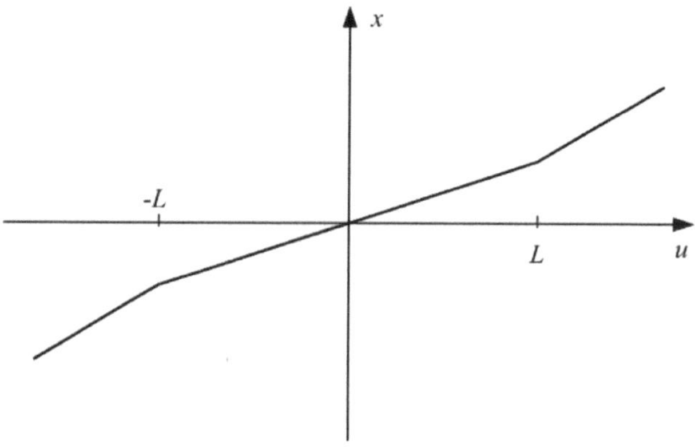

Figure 33:   The continuous version of the sculpting transformation

This example demonstrates how the continuity of the sculpting transformation can be achieved by a proper choice of the constants $o^x{}_k$. Note that the solution (7.4) is not unique; if $x(u)$ is a continuous transformation, so is

$$x'(u) = x(u) + c, \tag{7.5}$$

for any number c.

Let us demonstrate the effect of discontinuities in the sculpting transformation for a 1D assembly with a black-white primitive image cell:

Figure 34:   Black-white cell for the primitive image

The displayed images for non-continuous and continuous sculpting transformations are shown in Figure 35. The displayed cell width in region 2 is larger than its width in the other regions because it is higher, so it has a larger magnification. The tearing effect in the non-continuous transformation is clearly visible.

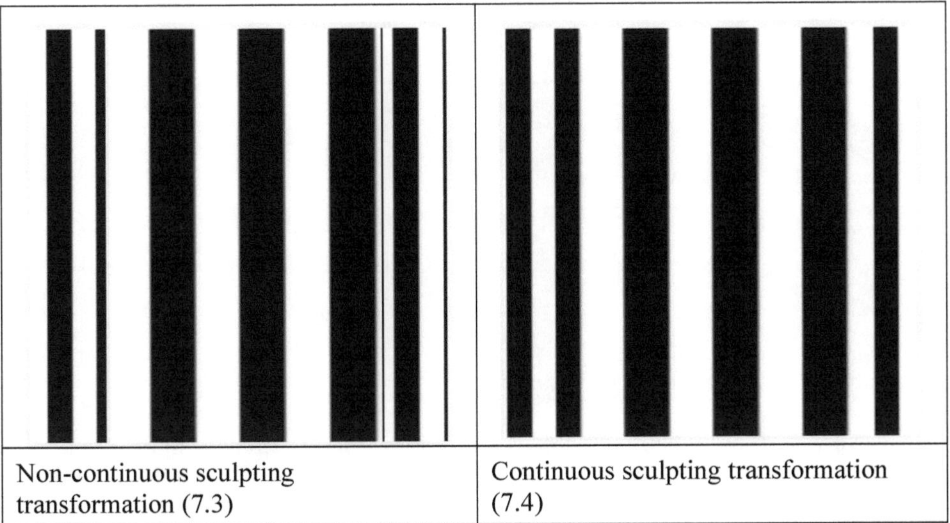

| Non-continuous sculpting transformation (7.3) | Continuous sculpting transformation (7.4) |

Figure 35:   Comparison of displayed images with non-continuous and continuous sculpting transformations

The derivation of the sculpting transformation for a general surface will rely on the principles outlined here. To continue, let us take a brief detour and introduce the concept of the staircase approximation.

7.3   The staircase approximation

Any surface can be approximated by planar patches parallel to the xy plane. Such an approximation is called "staircase approximation."

Figure 36 illustrates the staircase approximation in one dimension. It shows a continuous function $f(x)$ and its staircase approximation $f_\delta(x)$. The approximation is characterized by a step parameter δ. For a given segment, the value of $f_\delta(x)$ is the value of $f(x)$ at the segment's center.

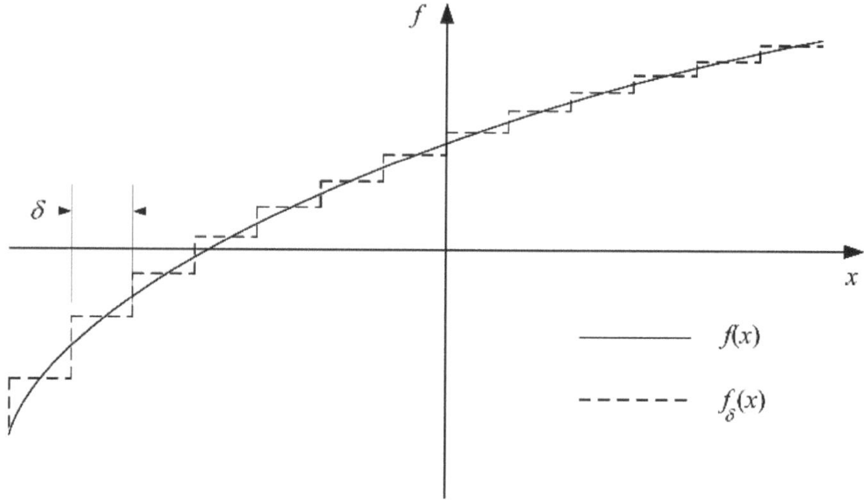

Figure 36:   The staircase approximation

The staircase approximation improves as the step becomes smaller. In the limit, it coincides with f:

$$\lim_{\delta \to 0} f_\delta(x) = f(x).$$

7.4   Derivation of the sculpting transformation

Let $h(\mathbf{u})$ be a height function defined on the backplane and let us divide the backplane into square tiles of size δ. A two-component index $\mathbf{k}$ will annotate each tile. The staircase approximation to h will be

$$h_\delta(\mathbf{u}) = h\left(c_{k(u)}\right) \quad \mathbf{u} \in D_{k(u)},$$

where $k(\boldsymbol{u})$ is the index of the tile containing the point $\boldsymbol{u}$, and $D_{k(u)}$ is its domain. The

point c_k is the center of the k'th tile. Note that, within each tile, the staircase

approximation is a plane parallel to the xy-plane. In the limit $\delta \to 0$, the tiles'
domains shrink to points, and the surface staircase approximation coincides with the
surface height function:

$$\lim_{\delta \to 0} h_\delta(\boldsymbol{u}) = h(\boldsymbol{u}).$$

The staircase sculpting transformation is derived by letting the projection point be at

a distance of $h_\delta(\boldsymbol{u})$ from the assembly front plane for each tile. This determines the z

coordinate of the projection point. Its plane coordinates in the front plane (or the
backplane, see (3.5)), are arbitrary. In fact, it is allowed to specify different plane
coordinates for the projection points of different tiles. However, within each tile, the
projection point coordinates must be constant.

For a given staircase approximation $h_\delta(\boldsymbol{u})$ of the height function $h(\boldsymbol{u})$, we can

define a corresponding staircase approximation to the projection constant:

$$\alpha_\delta(\boldsymbol{u}) = 1 + \frac{1}{h_\delta(\boldsymbol{u})}.$$

We can use the transformation (3.8) to define the staircase sculpting transformation:

$$\boldsymbol{x}_\delta(\boldsymbol{u}) = \frac{\boldsymbol{u}}{\alpha_\delta(\boldsymbol{u})} + \frac{\boldsymbol{o}^x_{k(u)}}{1 + h_\delta(\boldsymbol{u})}, \quad \boldsymbol{u} \in D_{k(u)} \tag{7.6}$$

where $k(\boldsymbol{u})$ is the index of the tile containing the point $\boldsymbol{u}$, and $D_{k(u)}$ is its domain. This

transformation includes an array of undetermined constants $\boldsymbol{o}_k$. These constants are

determined by the planar coordinates of the projection points, and as discussed above,
are arbitrary.

The staircase approximation is not continuous; the function $h_\delta(\boldsymbol{u})$ is non-

continuous even if $h(\boldsymbol{u})$ is. As demonstrated in sub-Chapter 7.2, the discontinuities in

the function $h_\delta(\boldsymbol{u})$ may create discontinuities in the corresponding sculpting

transformation $\boldsymbol{x}_\delta(\boldsymbol{u})$, unless the constants $\boldsymbol{o}^x_k$ are properly chosen.

We will derive the sculpting transformation from the staircase sculpting
transformations using a limiting process:

$$x(\boldsymbol{u}) = \lim_{\delta \to 0} x_\delta(\boldsymbol{u}). \tag{7.7}$$

In the limit, the discontinuities of the staircase sculpting transformations may disappear. However, the adverse effects of these discontinuities may remain. Therefore, to guarantee that (7.7) will yield a proper sculpting transformation, it is necessary that the staircase sculpting transformations be continuous.

7.5 Sculpting in one-dimensional assemblies

As discussed in sub-Chapter 6.1.6, the 3D moiré surface geometry in 1D assemblies is determined by the x-component of the sculpting transformation. For the sake of clarity, let us write explicitly the x-component of (7.6):

$$x_\delta(\boldsymbol{u}) = \frac{u}{\alpha_\delta(\boldsymbol{u})} + \frac{o^x_{k(u)}}{1 + h_\delta(\boldsymbol{u})}, \quad \boldsymbol{u} \in D_{k(u)}, \tag{7.8}$$

where x_δ is the x-component of $\boldsymbol{x}_\delta$ etc.

A continuous sculpting transformation for a staircase approximation can be derived using differential relations. Within each tile, the height is constant, so the derivatives of α_δ and h_δ vanish:

$$\frac{d\alpha_\delta}{du} = 0$$
$$\frac{dh_\delta}{du} = 0 \tag{7.9}$$

Furthermore, within each tile, o^x_k is constant too, so its derivatives also vanish. The staircase sculpting transformation equation is derived by differentiating (7.8) with respect to the backplane coordinate u:

$$\frac{dx_\delta}{du} = \frac{1}{\alpha_\delta(\boldsymbol{u})}. \tag{7.10}$$

The formal solution of (7.10) is

$$x_\delta(u,v) = \int \frac{du}{\alpha_\delta(u,v)} = \int \frac{h_\delta(u,v)}{1 + h_\delta(u,v)} du. \tag{7.11}$$

The staircase sculpting transformation $x_\delta(u)$, as defined in (7.11), is continuous, even though $\alpha_\delta(u)$ is non-continuous by the nature of the staircase approximation. This claim follows from the fact that

$$\lim_{\varepsilon \to 0} \int_x^{x+\varepsilon} f(x)\,dx = 0$$

even if the function $f(x)$ is not continuous. So, in the sculpting transformation defined by (7.11), the constants $o^x{}_k$ are automatically determined in such a way that the continuity of the transformation is guaranteed.

In the limit $\delta \to 0$, (7.10) yields the sculpting equation:

$$\frac{dx}{du} = \lim_{\delta \to 0} \frac{1}{\alpha_\delta(u)} = \frac{1}{\alpha(u)}\,, \tag{7.12}$$

with the formal solution

$$x(u,v) = \int \frac{h(u,v)}{1+h(u,v)}\,du. \tag{7.13}$$

7.6 Sculpting of two-dimensional assemblies

For the derivation of the sculpting transformation in 2D assemblies, we regard the backplane as a set of lines, rather than as a set of rectangular tiles. All lines intersect at the coordinates' origin, and each line is divided into segments of length δ. In the previous case, in which the backplane was divided into a set of square tiles, each tile was characterized by two indices. In the present case, each line segment is characterized by a single index k and a continuous angle θ. We will denote this characterization by a vector κ:

$$\kappa = (k,\theta).$$

The staircase approximation to the height function is defined as follows:

$$h_\delta(u) = h\big(c_{\kappa(u)}\big) \quad u \in D_{\kappa(u)}.$$

where $\kappa(u)$ is the index of the line segment containing the point u, and $D_{\kappa(u)}$ is its domain. The point c_κ is the center of the κ'th segment. Note that within each segment, the staircase approximation is a line parallel to the xy plane. This also defines the projection constant staircase approximation $\alpha_\delta\left(\boldsymbol{u}\right)$.

Let us consider a certain line segment $\boldsymbol{\kappa}$ with center $\boldsymbol{c}_\kappa$ and apply to it a projection transformation from a point located at height $h_\delta\left(\boldsymbol{c}_\kappa\right)$. Since the projection point is held constant for the whole segment, we can use (3.14)

$$\frac{dx_\delta}{dr} = \frac{\hat{\boldsymbol{r}}\left(\theta\right)}{\alpha_\delta\left(\boldsymbol{u}\right)} \tag{7.14}$$

to define the staircase sculpting transformation for the segment.

Equation (3.14) was derived under the assumption that the direction of the $\boldsymbol{o}$ vector in the projection point is the same as the direction of $\boldsymbol{u}$ (see (3.12)). This does not limit the present treatment, because as discussed in sub-Chapter 7.4, one can define arbitrarily a different vector $\boldsymbol{o}$ for each line segment, and, in particular, choose a vector $\boldsymbol{o}$ which is parallel to it.

The formal solution of (7.14) is

$$\boldsymbol{x}_\delta\left(r,\theta\right) = \int \frac{h_\delta\left(r,\theta\right)}{1+h_\delta\left(r,\theta\right)} dr \cdot \hat{\boldsymbol{r}}\left(\theta\right). \tag{7.15}$$

As discussed above, these transformations are continuous and, therefore, can be used to derive the sculpting transformation. In the limit $\delta \to 0$ we obtain

$$\boldsymbol{x}\left(r,\theta\right) = \int \frac{h\left(r,\theta\right)}{1+h\left(r,\theta\right)} dr \cdot \hat{\boldsymbol{r}}\left(\theta\right). \tag{7.16}$$

For the convenience of the reader, let us write down explicitly the Cartesian components of the sculpting transformation:

$$x_x\left(r,\theta\right) = \int \frac{h\left(r,\theta\right)}{1+h\left(r,\theta\right)} dr \cdot cos\,\theta,$$

$$x_y\left(r,\theta\right) = \int \frac{h\left(r,\theta\right)}{1+h\left(r,\theta\right)} dr \cdot sin\,\theta. \tag{7.17}$$

7.7   Surfaces defined on a finite domain

Our analysis applies to infinite assemblies (1.1 above). In the sculpting transformations, (7.13) and (7.16), it is assumed implicitly that the height function h is also defined on an infinite plane. In practice, the height function is often defined on a finite or a semi-infinite domain. Good examples of such functions are the hemi-cylindrical and hemi-spherical cases considered in 7.9.3 and 7.9.4 below.

Two problems arise when the definition domain of the height function is not infinite:

1. One may encounter undefined height values when attempting to compute the integrals in (7.13) and (7.16), making certain regions inaccessible for the computation,
2. Changes of finite domain boundaries with the viewing angle.

A universal solution to the first problem is to assign an arbitrary value, like h_0, to the height function wherever it is originally undefined. This solution technically works, but it creates arbitrary discontinuities in the surface. Such discontinuities may cause undesired visual effects.

Another approach is to break the surface into several disjoint sub-surfaces in such a manner that in each sub-surface, the integrals in (7.13) and (7.16) can be computed. This can be done in many cases, but it may also cause undesirable effects on the common boundaries of the sub-surfaces.

The position of the origin in the warping transformation calculation can be set to any location. Sometimes, inaccessible regions in 2D assemblies can be avoided by moving the coordinate origin. This method is illustrated schematically in Figure 37. The figure shows a circular domain in which the height function is defined on the circle, except for a small portion shown in black. The regions accessible for the transformation calculation are shown in blue, and those that are inaccessible are shown in red.

In part (a), the origin is at the circle's center. This choice creates an inaccessible region. Attempting to compute the transformation at a point A inside this region results in an integration path that passes through the undefined region (dashed line). This prevents the transformation of point A from being computed. In part (b), the origin is moved to the apex of the undefined region. In this case, the integration path to the same point A lies entirely within the defined region, so the transformation can be computed at this point. If applicable, this method is preferred over the others because it is less prone to visual defects.

In this context, the domain boundaries denote boundaries of imaged 3D objects. In a true 3D display, the object boundaries vary with the angle of view. Currently, it is unknown how to account for this effect in 3D moiré displays, and in the present formalism, the boundaries remain invariant across viewing angles. This introduces geometric distortion in the object's display. Loosely speaking, one may say that the displayed object's geometry appears flat, while its texture exhibits a 3D effect. We call such a display "pseudo-3D." Fortunately, this abnormality does not impact the effectiveness of the 3D illusion in most cases. Note: In the context of stereoscopic displays, "pseudo-3D" refers to a display in which the left and the right views are transposed. This is different from the present meaning.

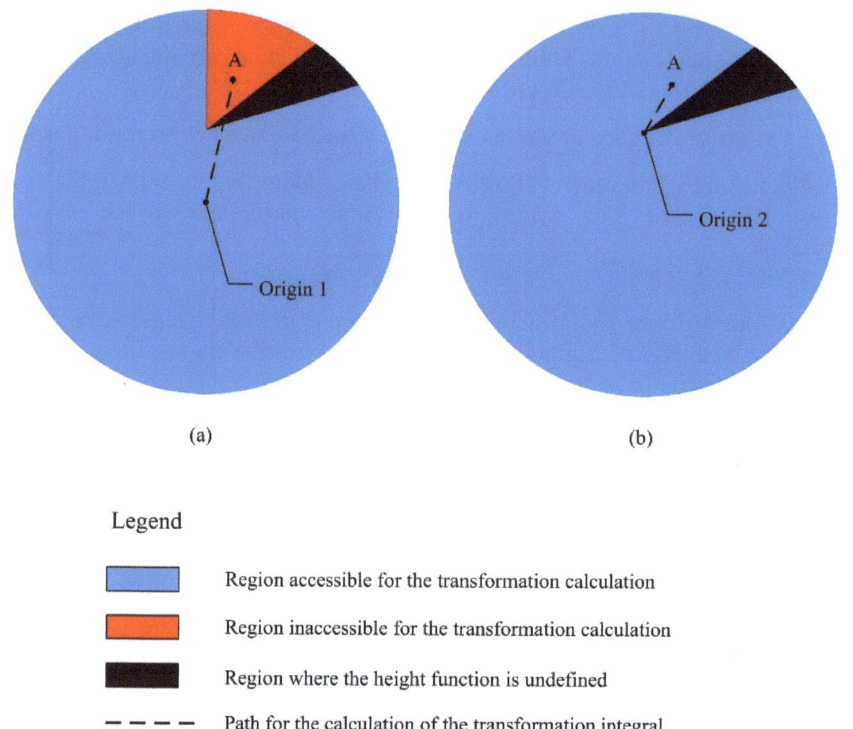

Figure 37: Elimination of the inaccessible zone by shifting the origin

7.8   Sculpting integrals

It is convenient to introduce a modified height function g:

$$g = 1 + h.\tag{7.18}$$

The modified height function differs from the original height function h by the reference: whereas h is measured from the front plane, g is measured from the backplane. It is easy to verify that

$$\frac{1}{\alpha} = 1 - \frac{1}{g}.$$

The formal solutions to the sculpting equations can be written in terms of the modified height function:

$$x(u,v) = u - \int \frac{du}{g(u,v)},\tag{7.19}$$

and

$$x(r,\theta) = \left[r - \int \frac{dr}{g(r,\theta)} \right] \cdot \hat{r}(\theta).$$

(7.20)

The calculation of the integrals appearing in (7.19) and (7.20) is the main effort in the derivation the sculpting transformations. These integrals measure the sculpting transformation amplitude, as they represent the differences between the transformed and the original points. In what follows, we will denote these integrals by I, and will call them "sculpting integrals:"

$$I_x(u,v) = \int \frac{du}{g(u,v)},$$

(7.21)

and

$$I_r(r,\theta) = \int \frac{dr}{g(r,\theta)}.$$

(7.22)

In principle, any surface with a unique height at any given backplane point can be treated by this formalism. This includes non-continuous surfaces as well.

If the height function is specified analytically, one may attempt to derive analytic formulas for the sculpting transformation (see examples below). Analytical formulas bring the advantage of computational speed and precision. If analytical integration is impractical, it is always possible to resort to numerical methods.

Surfaces can be defined numerically by a table specifying the height function at an array of points. Often one can find an analytic approximation to a surface specified in this manner. If the resulting sculpting integrals have a known analytic representation, it is possible to obtain analytic sculpting transformations in this case too.

7.9   Examples

7.9.1   General

There are many examples of height functions which are amenable to analytic integration. Here, we will discuss two cases of particular importance:

- Linear: inclined plane and cone

- Spheroid: hemi-sphere and hemi-cylinder

For the linear case, we will use the analytic formula

$$\int \frac{du}{au+b} = \frac{1}{a} ln\left(1 + \frac{au}{b} \right) + c.$$

(7.23)

For the spheroid case, we will use the analytic formula

$$\int \frac{du}{\sqrt{1 - z^2 \left(u^2 + v^2\right)}} = \frac{1}{z} tan^{-1} \left(\frac{zu}{\sqrt{1 - z^2 \left(u^2 + v^2\right)}} \right) + c. \qquad (7.24)$$

For the case $v = 0$, this formula simplifies to

$$\int \frac{du}{\sqrt{1 - z^2 u^2}} = \frac{1}{z} sin^{-1} \left(zu \right) + c. \qquad (7.25)$$

In Chapter 6 we discussed the limitations on the imaging volume. In the examples below, these limitations are ignored. In practice, this can be done if no numerical singularities arise. As for any potential visual defects, they can be best judged by experiment.

7.9.2   Linear modified height function

In one-dimensional assemblies, the linear modified height function is given by:

$$g = au + b.$$

Using (7.23), the sculpting integral for this case is

$$I_x \left(u, v \right) = \frac{1}{a} ln \left(1 + \frac{au}{b} \right) + c. \qquad (7.26)$$

All three quantities (a, b, c) appearing in (7.26) may depend on v. This case can be used to represent a general inclined plane.

In two-dimensional assemblies, the linear modified height function is given by:

$$g = ar + b.$$

With constant a and b this function represents a cone whose apex is on the z-axis. Using (7.23), the sculpting integral for this case is

$$I_r \left(r \right) = \int \frac{dr}{ar + b} = \frac{1}{a} ln \left(1 + \frac{ar}{b} \right) + c. \qquad (7.27)$$

In general, all three quantities (a, b, c) appearing in (7.26) may depend on θ, in which case the surface will not be a cone.

7.9.3   Hemi-cylindrical surface

The hemi-cylinder is an example of a more complicated surface for which a simple analytic solution exists. However, it is also of great importance in practical applications. The hemi-cylindrical surface used in the present example is shown in

Figure 38. Note that the cylinder axis lies in the backplane of the assembly and coincides with the v axis.

In the one-dimensional assemblies the height function of this surface is given by

$$H(u) = \sqrt{R^2 - u^2} - t, \quad |u| \le R. \tag{7.28}$$

The height function value for a certain arbitrary point a is shown in Figure 38. The modified height function g (7.18) for this case is

$$g(u) = \frac{R}{t}\sqrt{1 - \left(\frac{u}{R}\right)^2}. \tag{7.29}$$

Using (7.25), we get

$$I_x(u) = \frac{t}{R}\int \frac{du}{\sqrt{1 - \left(\frac{u}{R}\right)^2}} = t\,sin^{-1}\left(\frac{u}{R}\right) + c. \tag{7.30}$$

This can also be written as

$$I_x(u) = -t\theta(u) + c', \tag{7.31}$$

where the angle θ is defined in Figure 38. Note that in this case, the integrand in (7.30) is singular at $u = R$, but the sculpting integral itself is not.

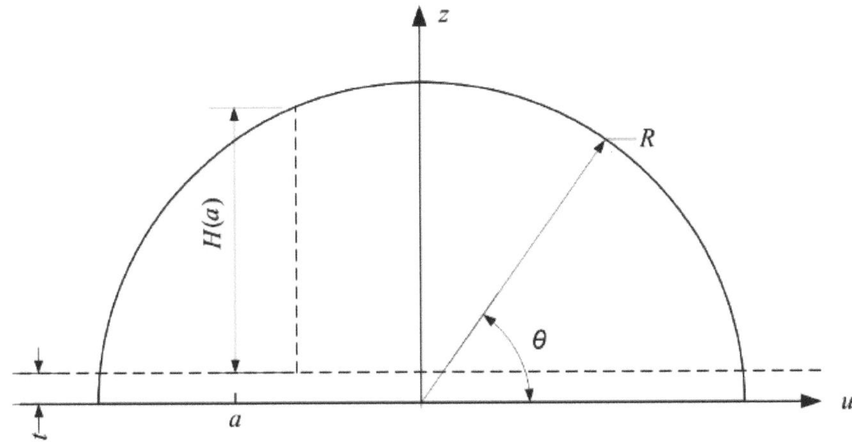

Figure 38: The hemi-cylindrical surface

In two-dimensional assemblies, the height function is expressed in polar coordinates:

$$H(r,\theta) = \sqrt{R^2 - r^2 \cos^2 \theta} - t, \quad r \leq R. \tag{7.32}$$

The modified height function g (7.18) for this case is

$$g(r) = \frac{R}{t}\sqrt{1 - \left(\frac{r \cos \theta}{R}\right)^2}. \tag{7.33}$$

To calculate the sculpting integral for this case, we use again (7.25) and obtain

$$I_r(r,\theta) = \frac{t}{R}\int \frac{dr}{\sqrt{1 - \left(\dfrac{r \cos \theta}{R}\right)^2}} = t \sin^{-1}\left(\frac{r \cos \theta}{R}\right) + c. \tag{7.34}$$

7.9.4 Hemi-spherical surface

The hemi-spherical surface is shown in Figure 39. For one-dimensional assemblies the corresponding height function is expressed as

$$H(u,v) = \sqrt{R^2 - u^2 - v^2} - t, \quad u^2 + v^2 \leq R^2.$$

The modified height function g (7.18) for this case is

$$g(u,v) = \frac{R}{t}\sqrt{1 - \frac{u^2 + v^2}{R^2}}.$$

To calculate sculpting integral for this case, we use (7.24), and obtain

$$I_x(u,v) = \frac{t}{R}\int \frac{du}{\sqrt{1 - \left(\dfrac{u^2 + v^2}{R^2}\right)}} = t \tan^{-1}\left(\frac{u}{\sqrt{R^2 - \left(u^2 + v^2\right)}}\right) + c.$$

$$\tag{7.35}$$

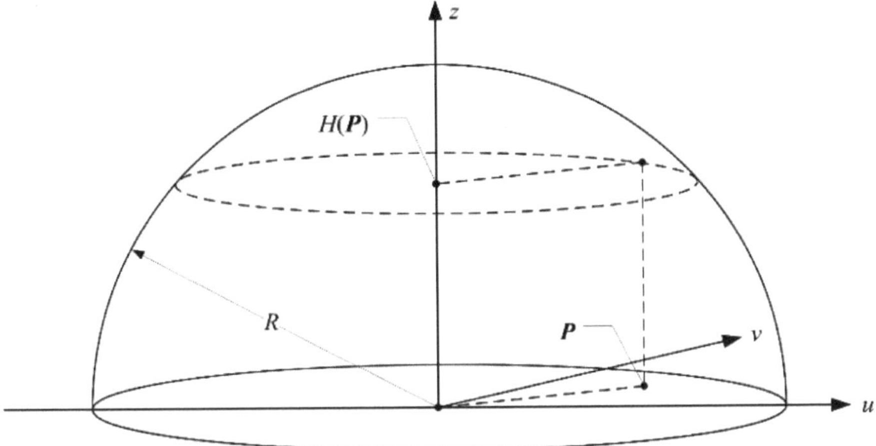

Figure 39: Hemi-spherical surface geometry

For two-dimensional assemblies, we consider the hemi-spherical surface in cylindrical coordinates as shown in Figure 40.

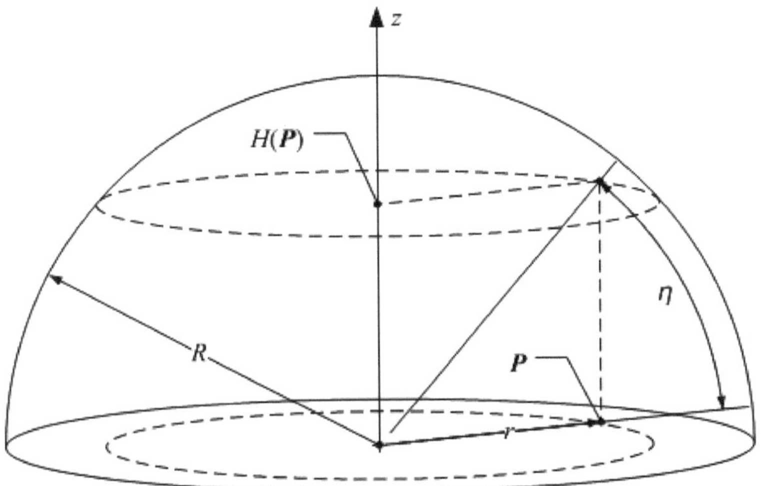

Figure 40: The spherical surface in cylindrical coordinates

The height function in this case is given by

$$H(r) = \sqrt{R^2 - r^2} - t, \quad r \le R.$$ (7.36)

The modified height function g (7.18) for this case is

$$g(r) = \frac{R}{t}\sqrt{1 - \left(\frac{r}{R}\right)^2} \; . \tag{7.37}$$

Using (7.25), the sculpting integral in this case is

$$I_r(r) = \frac{t}{R}\int \frac{du}{\sqrt{1 - \left(\dfrac{r}{R}\right)^2}} = t\,sin^{-1}\left(\frac{r}{R}\right) + c \; . \tag{7.38}$$

This can also be written as

$$I_r(r) = -t\eta(r) + c' \, , \tag{7.39}$$

where the angle η is the latitude angle of point P, as defined in Figure 40. Note that in this case, the integrand in the sculpting integral (7.38) is singular at $r = R$, but the sculpting integral itself is not.

8 THE LENTICULAR MOIRÉ ASSEMBLY

8.1 Main characteristics

The lenticular moiré assembly is a one-dimensional optical assembly made from a lenticular sheet, which is an array of cylindrical plano-convex lenses called "lenticules." The correct 3D geometry of the moiré surface can be seen only when the viewer's ocular vector is perpendicular to the lenticules direction. For this reason, lenticular assemblies designed to be hung on a wall are oriented with the lenticules in the vertical direction.

In lenticular moiré assemblies the displayed image fully covers the picture area, without vacancies. Due to this property, the displayed image in such assemblies has a high visual quality. In addition, the sampling is very sharp and allows a high-resolution display of the cell graphics.

The visual resolution element of the displayed image in the horizontal direction is the lenticule width. In the vertical direction the image displays the cell graphics as is, so the visual resolution element in this direction is the printing resolution. The cell graphics can be arbitrarily transformed in the vertical direction without affecting the moiré surface geometry. This property can be used to create additional visual effects.

8.2 The lenticular sheet

All lenticules in a lenticular sheet share a common backplane, which also serves as the backplane of the assembly. The lenses are deposited with zero gaps between them, thus covering the whole sheet surface. A photograph of a lenticular sheet is shown in Figure 41.

Figure 41: A lenticular sheet

The lenticule is a union of a solid cuboid and a cylindrical section (Figure 42). The axis is the center of the parent cylinder, and is an imaginary object that cannot be seen.

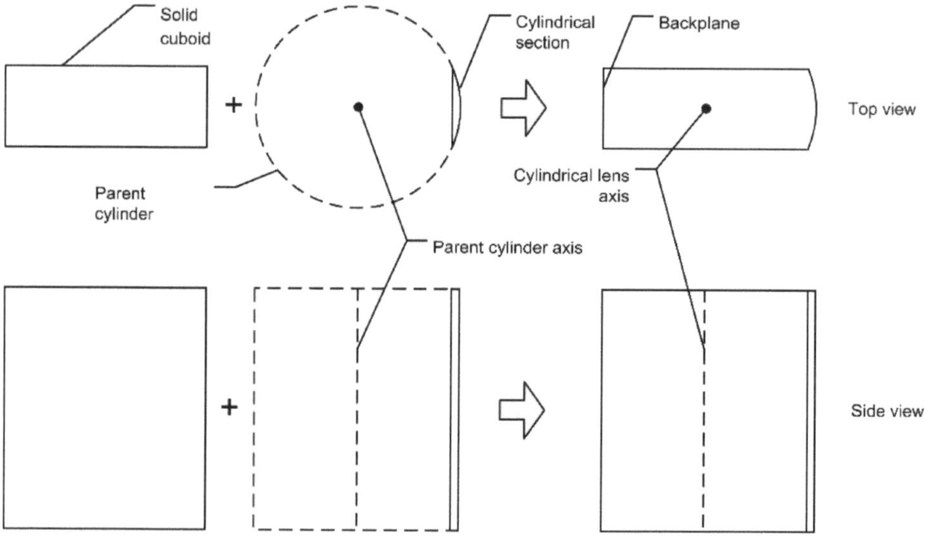

Figure 42: Lenticule geometry (Weissman, Lenticular Imaging, 2018)

The lenticular sheet cross-section is shown schematically in Figure 43. There is one axis per lenticule. All axes are parallel and lie in the same plane, which is the assembly front plane.

Two physical characteristics of the lenticular sheet are important in the analysis: the inter-axial separation p and the distance t between the front plane and the backplane. Both are shown in Figure 43. The coordinate system is chosen so that the axes are parallel to the y axis.

The sheet thickness is denoted in Figure 43 by t'. The value of the planes separation parameter t depends on the lenticule optical design. Often, the lenticules are designed to focus rays from infinity (parallel rays) on the backplane. In such cases (Weissman, Lenticular Imaging, 2018)

$$t = \frac{t'}{n},$$

where n is the sheet index of refraction.

8.3   Cells and grids

In lenticular assemblies, the front plane is embedded inside the sheet (see Figure 43). The front plane cells are bounded by the boundaries of the lenticules and are shown in Figure 43 as dashed-dotted lines. These cells are bands of width p extending to infinity.

In the center of every cell, there is an axis, which also serves as the cell center object. The front plane grid is the set of all axes, and is an equidistant grid of the kind discussed in sub-Chapters 2.4 and 2.5. The sampling grid is the projection of the axes on the backplane from the viewing point.

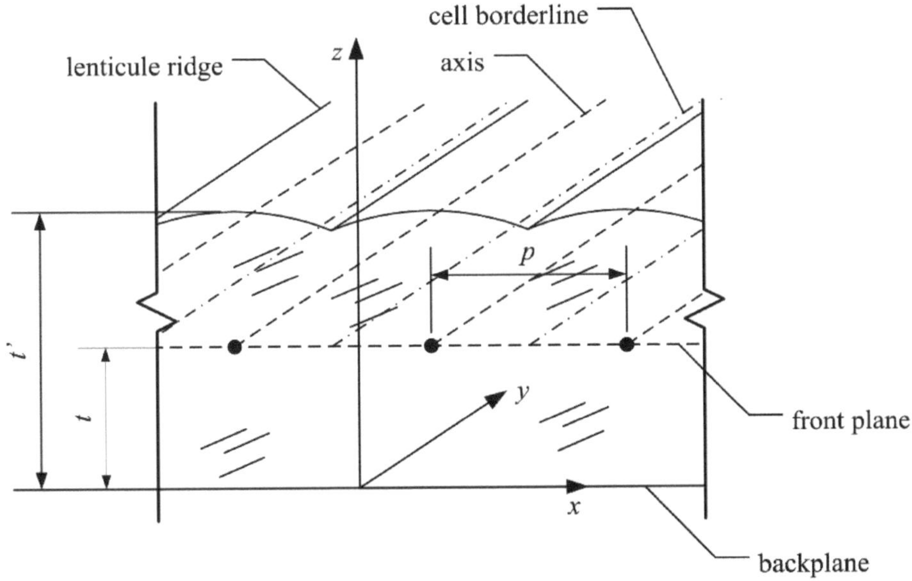

Figure 43:   The lenticular sheet scheme

8.4   Image forming in a lenticular moiré assembly

The general discussion of sub-Chapter 4.2 applies to lenticular moiré assemblies. Here, we will present the imaging mechanism characteristic of lenticular sheets.

The sampled graphics of a single lenticule is simply the graphics of the backplane image, which overlaps its sampling gridline. Mathematically, the sampled graphics of a lenticule is a color function defined on a line.

The image-forming mechanism of a given lenticule consists of expanding the sampled graphics in the x direction until it fills out the lenticule aperture. The image displayed by a lenticule is independent of x but generally varies with y. The sampling and the image-forming mechanisms for a single lenticule are illustrated in Figure 44.

The lenticular imaging processes occur independently and simultaneously in all lenticules. Since the lenticules' apertures cover the whole plane without any voids, the image displayed by all lenticules also covers the entire plane. This is the displayed image of the lenticular moiré assembly.

Since the position of the sampling line depends on the viewing point, the lenticule will, in general, display different graphics for different viewing points. This effect is illustrated in the two photographs shown in Figure 45. In these photographs, a lenticular sheet was placed on a vertical line whose thickness is approximately 1/3 of the lenticule width. In picture (a), the position of the sampling line is outside the drawn line, and therefore, the lenticule does not display it. In (b), the camera was moved to make the sampling line overlap the drawn line. This time, the lenticule displays the drawn line. Note that the displayed line width is expanded to the width of the lenticule.

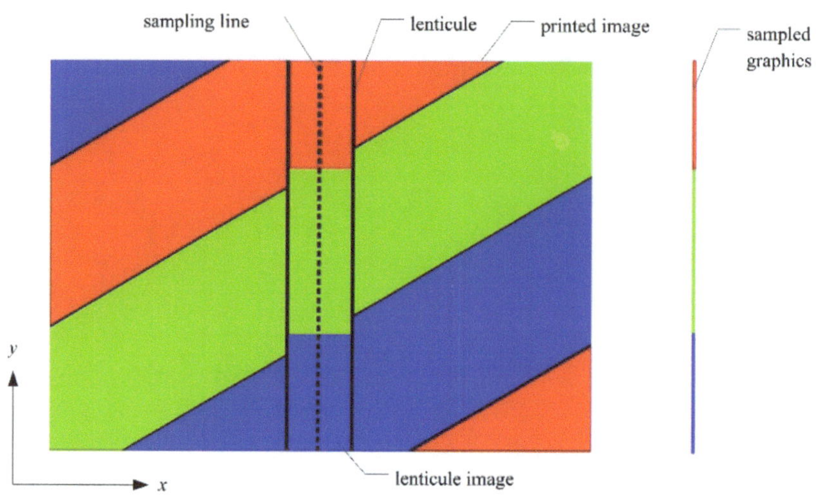

Figure 44:   The optical effect of a lenticule

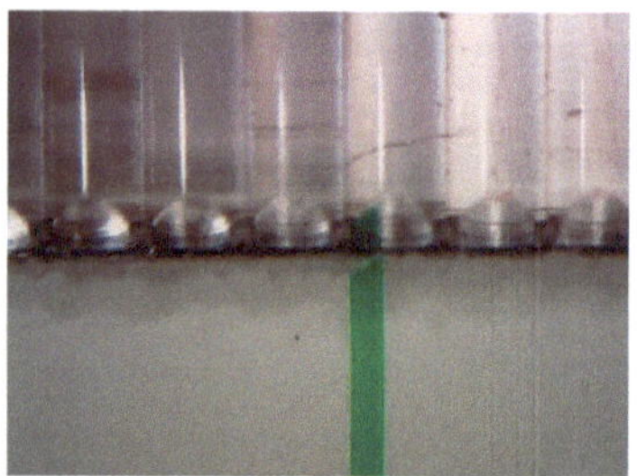

Figure 45:   The effect of viewing point motion on the lenticule display. left: the sampling line is outside the drawn line, right: the sampling line overlaps the drawn line

Another illustration of the lenticule optical effect is shown in Figure 46 (Weissman, Lenticular Imaging, 2018). Here, a small lenticular sheet was superimposed on a line at a certain angle.

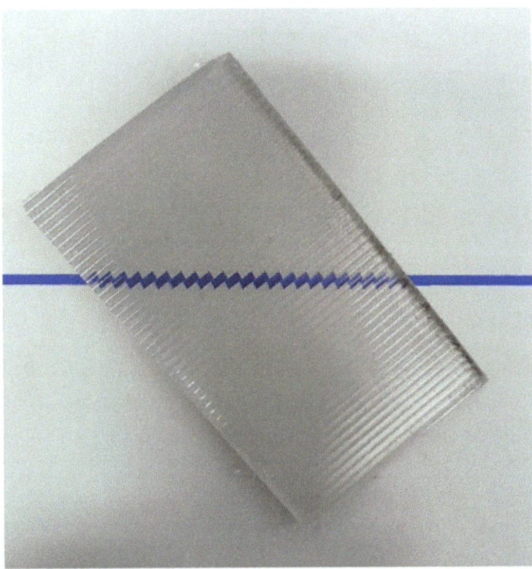

Figure 46:　The optical effect of a lenticular sheet superimposed on a slanted line

8.5　Magnification considerations

The backplane image in lenticular assemblies is made by printing. Printers have a finite resolution; therefore, the printer can resolve only a certain minimal pixel size p_x. Let us assume that the backplane image is printed at the maximal printer resolution, so that its pixel size equals p_x. A printed pixel is displayed magnified laterally by M, so the displayed pixel lateral size will be

$$S_x = |M| p_x. \tag{8.1}$$

As explained in sub-Chapter 8.4, the smallest horizontal resolution element in the displayed image is the lenticule width p. In order to display the picture at full resolution, it must be designed so that

$$S_x \geq p, \tag{8.2}$$

or, in other words, the magnification must satisfy:

$$|M| \geq \frac{p}{p_x}. \tag{8.3}$$

Equation (8.3) can be written in terms that are more common in the art. The parameter that determines the pixel size in the printer's driver is the printing density. This parameter is traditionally measured in units of pixels per inch, a unit called "ppi." The lenticule width p is the inverse of the lenticules density, which is also traditionally expressed in lenticules per inch ("lpi"). Let γ be a printing density value which corresponds to a pixel size of p_x

$$\gamma = \frac{1}{p_x},$$

and let l be the lpi value of the lenticular sheet. Equation (8.3) can now be written as

$$|M| \geq \frac{\gamma}{l}. \tag{8.4}$$

For example, it is commonly accepted that the maximum printing density that yields resolvable pixels for Epson Stylus inkjet printers is 720dpi. So, for a lenticular sheet of 20lpi, the magnification should satisfy

$$|M| \geq \frac{720}{20} = 36.$$

The printed pixels become visually resolved when

$$|M| > \frac{\gamma}{l} \tag{8.5}$$

A picture that resolves the printed pixels may exhibit undesired visual features. Therefore, one should avoid magnifications much greater than the right-hand side of (8.5). Following these considerations, the optimal magnification values M_o are given by

$$M_o = \pm \frac{\gamma}{l}. \tag{8.6}$$

8.6 The imaging volume of a lenticular 3D moiré surface

For a large enough viewing distance, the magnification is equal to the normalized height with a reversed sign (4.18). This observation allows us to translate the limitations on the magnification to constraints on the displayed depth. Let us define the optimal depths as follows:

$$|H_0| = |M_0|t$$

Constraining the displayed image depths to $\pm|H_0|$ will allow imaging on just two planes, one in front and the other behind the picture plane, as shown in Figure 47.

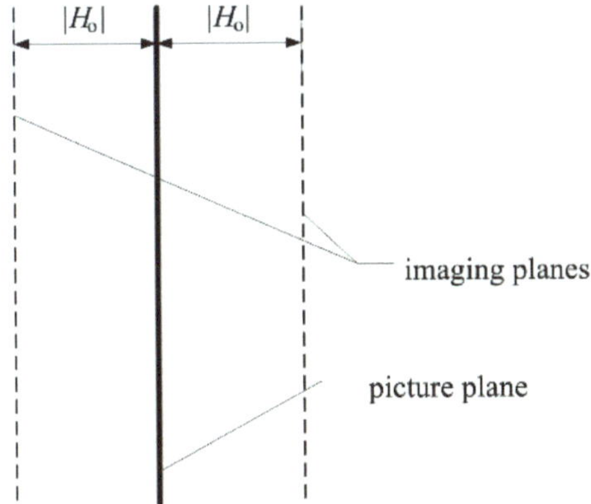

Figure 47:   Imaging on optimal planes

Three-dimensional sculpting requires a certain range of depth. One can, for instance, decide that the following range of depths is acceptable:

$$\frac{|H_o|}{2} < |H| < 2|H_o|. \tag{8.7}$$

Such constraint creates a certain volume for imaging, as illustrated in Figure 48. This figure also shows the forbidden zone, which, according to (6.16) contains collapsed grid singularities.

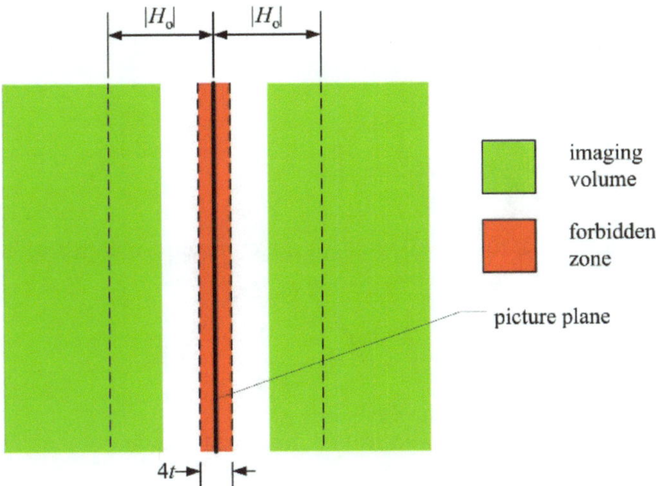

Figure 48:   Imaging volume corresponding to (8.7)

8.7   Sphere/cylinder imaging considerations

A cross-section of a hemi-spherical/cylindrical surface in the $z \times u$ plane is shown schematically in Figure 49. The magnified cell size is denoted by a, and the surface radius by R. The angle θ is given by

$$\theta \approx \frac{a}{R},\tag{8.8}$$

and the number of cells N_c on the (hemi-sphere/cylinder) surface is

$$N_c = \frac{\pi}{\theta} \approx \frac{\pi R}{a}.\tag{8.9}$$

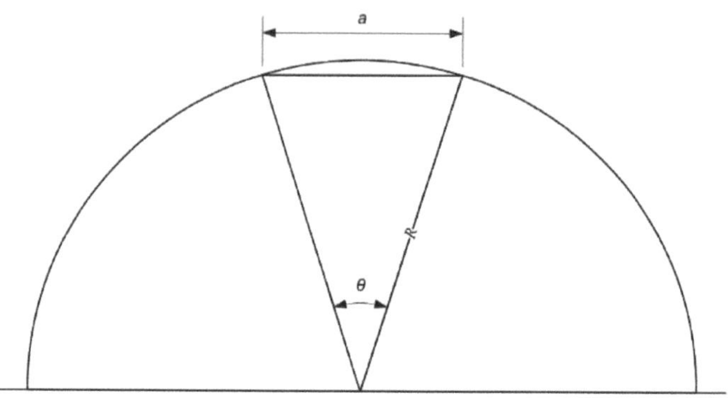

Figure 49:   3D moiré imaging on a sphere/cylinder surface

The magnified cell size is

$$a = |M|\, p_b,$$

where p_b is the backplane image cell width at the cylinder center. Since this cell is designed to be displayed at height R, its value is

$$p_b = \alpha_R p = \left(1 + \frac{t}{R}\right) p.\tag{8.10}$$

Assuming that the picture is viewed from a distance much larger than R, we can use (4.18) to approximate M:

$$|M| = \frac{R}{t}.\tag{8.11}$$

From (8.8) it follows that

$$\theta = \frac{p}{t}\left(1 + \frac{t}{R}\right) \approx \frac{p}{t},$$
(8.12)

where it was assumed that $R >> t$. The approximated value of θ does not depend on the surface radius R.

The angle θ, as given by (8.12), is approximately the sheet viewing angle (Weissman, Lenticular Imaging, 2018). The typical viewing angle of lenticular lenses designed for 3D imaging is ~0.5 radians. Therefore, by (8.12), the number of cells imaged on a hemi-sphere/cylinder surface with such a lens will be approximately 2π, regardless of the surface radius.

According to (8.7), a reasonable choice for the radius is

$$R \approx 2|M_o|t.$$
(8.13)

Let us consider a concrete example. A common lens for 3D lenticular imaging has a lenticule density of 20 lpi (lenticules per inch) with a thickness of 3mm and an index of refraction of ~1.5. The value of t for this lens is ~2 mm. The printing density that can be achieved with Epson Stylus inkjet printers is 720 ppi. This gives an optimal value of ~144 mm for R.

8.8   Designing the displayed image graphics

8.8.1   Design principles

When it comes to one-dimensional assemblies, the moiré magnification is not uniform and only affects the horizontal axis. As a result, the displayed image cells may look distorted compared to the original primitive image cells. To ensure that the graphics are displayed correctly, a specific design process needs to be followed.

Special software is needed to create the backplane image for the lenticular assembly. The input to such software will be the primitive image cell graphics. Here we will use examples to show how to design this cell to achieve the desired effect in three different applications.

The geometry of an image is characterized by its aspect, which is defined as

$$a = \frac{W}{U},$$

where W and U are the image width and height, respectively. Let the desired aspect of the displayed graphics be a_d, and its aspect in the backplane image cell be a_b. Since the moiré magnification acts only horizontally,

$$a_d = Ma_b.$$

Therefore, to achieve the desired aspect, the graphics in the backplane image must have the aspect

$$a_b = \frac{a_d}{M}.$$

The graphics width in the backplane cannot exceed the backplane cell width, which is p_b. Usually, the backplane graphics is designed to fill the whole backplane image cell width. Assuming that this is the case, the graphics height Z in the backplane image will be

$$Z = \frac{p_b}{a_b} = \frac{Mp_b}{a_d}. \tag{8.14}$$

In most cases $p_b \approx p$, and one can use the approximate formula instead:

$$Z \approx \frac{p}{a_b} = \frac{Mp}{a_d}. \tag{8.15}$$

However, in the examples below, we will use (8.14). We will ignore the slight magnification in the vertical direction caused by the projection of the primitive image. In this approximation, the size of the primitive image cell should be $p \times Z$.

We will use the image shown in Figure 50 [after (Tedliashvili, 2021)] for the examples. The dimensions of this image are normalized to its height. The aspect of this image is 0.3. We will use the parameters shown in Table 3 for the examples. Until now, we assumed that the lenticular assembly extends to infinity in the x and y directions. The following examples are intended for practical cases; therefore, here we make an exception and assign finite dimensions to the moiré assembly.

Table 3:   Picture parameters used in the example

Parameter	Units	Value
Moiré assembly width	mm	200
Moiré assembly height	mm	200
Lens lpi	1/inch	20
Planes gap	mm	3
Required aspect ratio	-	0.3

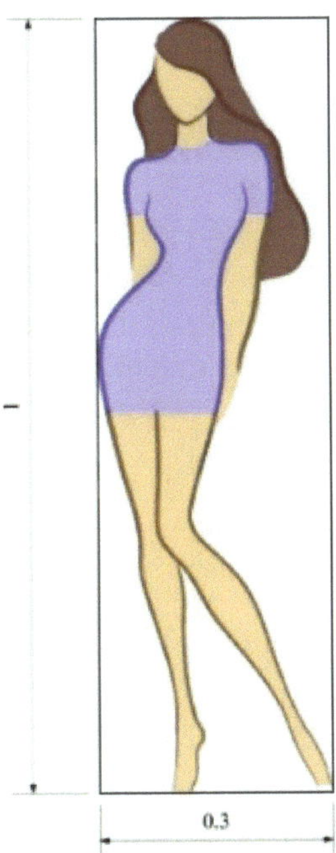

Figure 50:   Image for the examples

For each example, we will show an illustration of the displayed image. These illustrations are not photographs of actual pictures, but rather computer emulations.

8.8.2   Example: cell design for imaging on a plane

Let us design the primitive image cell for display on a plane protruding at 60mm from the picture plane. Assuming that the viewing distance is much larger than 60mm, the magnification will be (4.18)

$$M = -\frac{60}{3} = -20.$$

The primitive image cell width is

$$p = \frac{25.4}{20} = 1.27 \text{ mm}.$$

The projection constant for projection from 60 mm is

$$\alpha_h = 1 + \frac{3}{60} = 1.05.$$

Accordingly, the backplane image cell width is

$$p_b = \alpha_h p = 1.33 \text{ mm.}$$

According to (8.14), the backplane image graphics height should be

$$Z = \frac{Mp_b}{a_d} = \frac{20 \cdot 1.33}{0.3} = 88.7 \text{ mm.}$$

The required graphics size in the primitive image should be 1.27mm x 88.7mm, with an aspect of 0.014. The primitive image graphics are obtained by resizing the original image to the required dimensions.

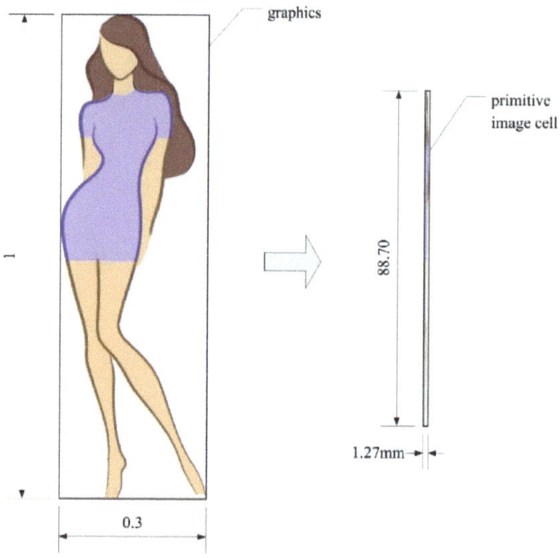

Figure 51:   The primitive image cell for imaging on a plane

Since the assembly height is 200 mm (Table 4), there is room for two images stacked vertically. The emulation of the resulting displayed image is shown in Figure 52. Note that the cell image is reversed with respect to the original graphics because the magnification is negative.

The graphics in Figure 52 have the correct aspect. This validates the correctness of the design process explained here.

Figure 52:   The displayed image imaged on a plane

8.8.3   Example: cell design for imaging on a hemi-sphere

Let us consider here an example of how to design a lenticular 3D moiré picture with a hemi-spherical surface. We will use the same parameters and graphics as in the plane example. In the present example, there is one additional parameter, the sphere radius, which we will assume to be 80mm. The picture front and side views are shown schematically in Figure 53 and Figure 54, respectively.

In the case of the moiré assembly with a planar displayed image, the magnification was constant. In the present case, the magnification will vary and be highest at the surface center. This raises the question of what magnification should be used for the cell design.

The best magnification choice for the cell design is the height of a region on the surface that is parallel to the assembly plane. In the present case, it is the magnification of the surface center. One may imagine a plane parallel to the assembly plane and tangent to the hemisphere at its center. The cell should be designed as if it is to be displayed on this plane. This plane is shown in Figure 54 and labeled "design plane." The height of this plane is 80mm, so the value of the projection constant at the center is

$$\alpha_c = 1 + \frac{t}{R} = 1.0375,$$

and the corresponding magnification is

$$M_c = -\frac{R}{t} = -26.67.$$

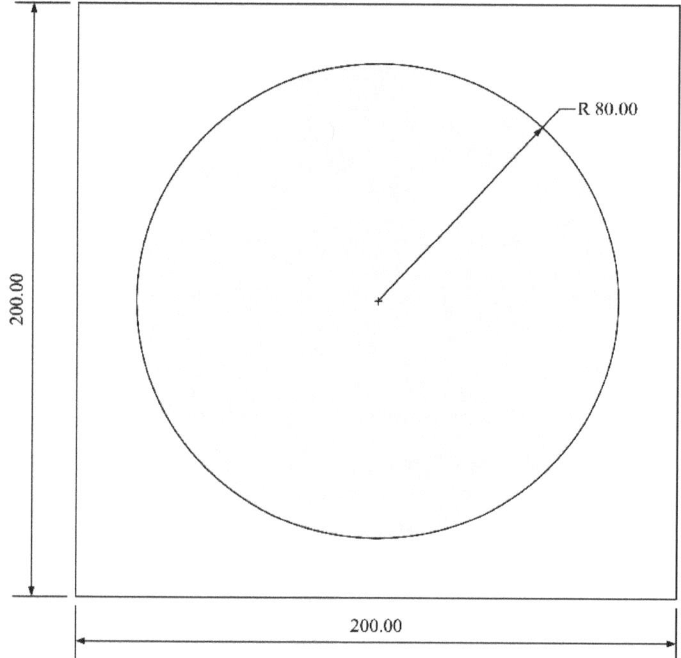

Figure 53:   Scheme of the picture in the example

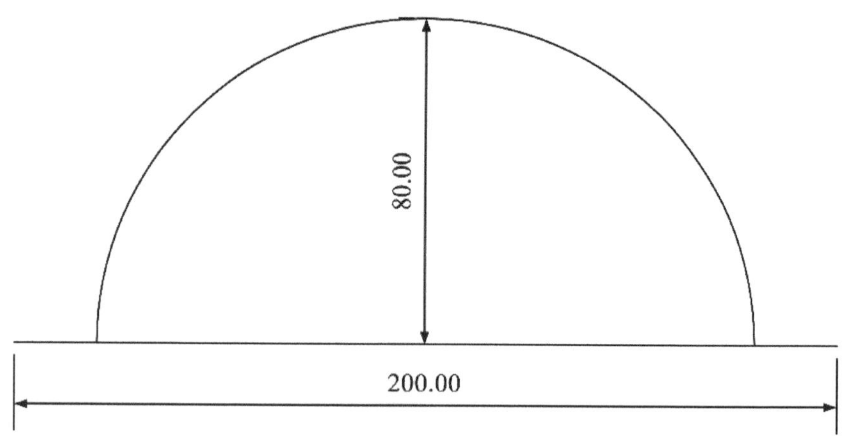

Figure 54:   Picture side view with the moiré surface

The backplane image cell width at the center is

$$p_c = \alpha_c p = 1.32 \text{ mm.}$$

By (8.14), the backplane graphics height should be

$$Z = \frac{|M_c|\, p_c}{a_d} = 117 \text{ mm.}$$

The primitive image cell for this example will have dimensions of $p \times Z$, which in this case are $1.27 \text{ mm} \times 117 \text{ mm}$. This cell is illustrated in Figure 55. Since the diameter is 160 mm, there is no room for two images stacked vertically, as in the plane example.

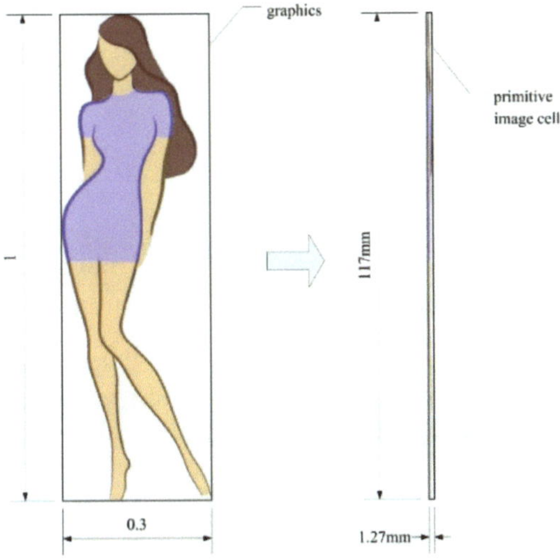

Figure 55:   The original graphics and the primitive image cell

A simulated view of the displayed image is shown in Figure 56.

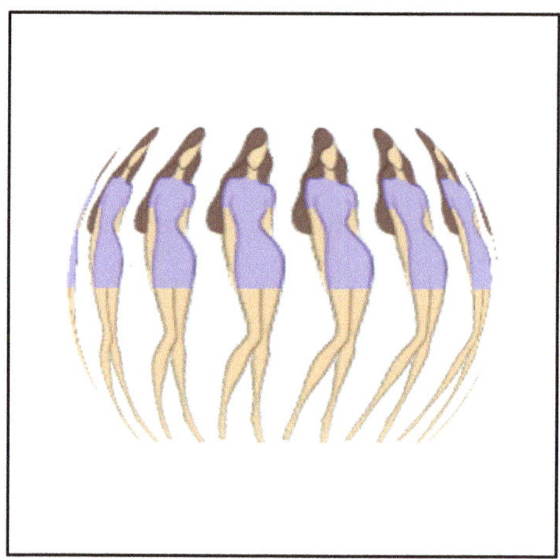

Figure 56:   The displayed image for the hemispherical surface

8.8.4   Example: cell design for imaging on a hemi-cylinder

We will use the sphere radius of the previous example (80mm) as the cylinder radius in the present example. In such a case, the hemi-sphere primitive cell is used for the hemi-cylinder surface. The cylinder height is set to 160mm, so there is no room for two vertically stacked images. The displayed image for this case is shown in Figure 57.

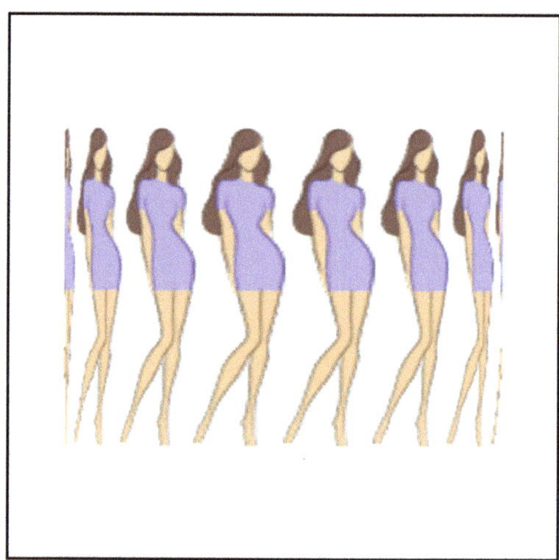

Figure 57:   The displayed image for the hemicylinder surface

8.8.5 Bars cell

Sometimes, the purpose of the cell graphics is not to display a graphical object but rather to reveal the geometry of the 3D moiré surface. A cell which is an array of alternating bars, as shown in Figure 58, is adequate for this purpose. In this example, the bar colors are black and white, but they can be any color. Figure 59 shows a moiré view of this cell applied to a cylindrical surface.

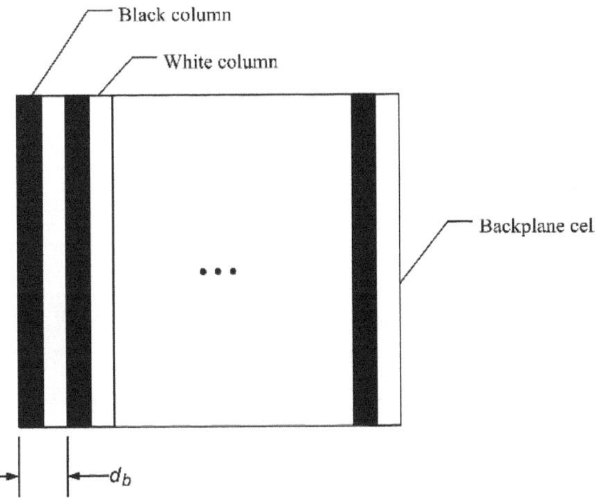

Figure 58: Alternating bars cell

Figure 59: A cylindrical surface with the bars cell

In this application, one often desires to make the bars as dense as possible. Let us see what the consequences of this requirement are.

The minimal width of a column is the resolved printed pixel size p_x (8.5 above). Therefore, the minimum distance between adjacent black columns (d_b in Figure 58) is

$$d_b = 2p_x = \frac{2}{\gamma},$$

where γ is the maximal resolved printing density (8.5 above). Let us assume that the picture is designed for the optimal magnification M_0 (8.6). In such a case, the displayed distance between adjacent black columns d_v will be

$$d_v = |M_o|d_b = \frac{\gamma}{l}\frac{2}{\gamma} = \frac{2}{l},$$

where l is the lpi value of the lenticular sheet. However,

$$\text{lenticule width} = \frac{1}{l}.$$

Therefore, in this example, the distance between adjacent black columns is two lenticules. This is the minimum distance achievable with optimal magnification.

9 THE FLY-EYE MOIRÉ ASSEMBLY

9.1 The fly-eye sheet

The fly-eye sheet is an array of spherical plano-convex lenses called lenslets. All lenses share a common backplane, which is the backplane of the sheet.

The lenses are arranged in a two-dimensional lattice, which may have different geometries. The most common geometries are square and hexagonal. Photographs of UV printed sheets (Droptix basics, 2022) in two geometries are shown in Figure 60 and Figure 61.

The photographs show that the spherical surfaces have circular boundaries and do not cover the whole sheet surface. In such circumstances, it is convenient to regard the lenslet as having a cylindrical body (Figure 62). The lenslets are embedded in an optical window with the same index of refraction as the lenses. The hexagonal lattice has a much higher area coverage percentage and therefore offers better visual quality.

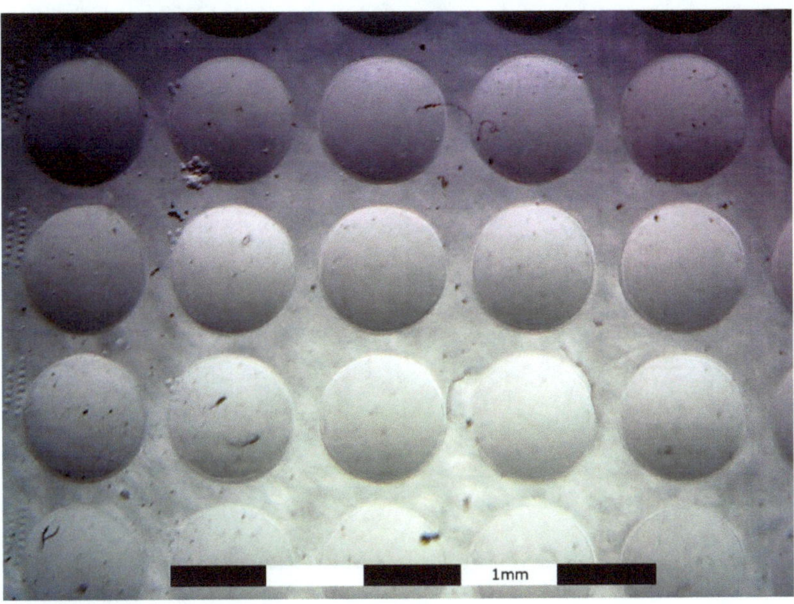

Figure 60: Fly-eye sheet in square geometry

Figure 61: Fly-eye sheet in hexagonal geometry

The lenslet geometry is shown in Figure 62. It is a union of a cylinder and a ball section. The lens center plays a similar role to the lenticule axis. It is a virtual and invisible object.

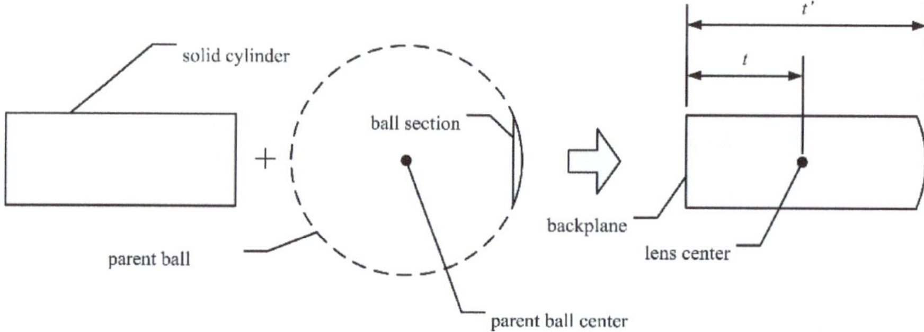

Figure 62: Lens geometry

The sheet thickness is denoted in Figure 62 by t'. Often, the lenses are designed to focus rays from infinity on the backplane. In such cases (Weissman, Lenticular Imaging, 2018)

$$t = \frac{t'}{n},$$

where t is the distance from the lens center to the backplane, and n is the sheet index of refraction.

9.2   The fly-eye assembly objects

As in the lenticular case, the front plane of the fly-eye sheet is embedded within the sheet and located a distance t from the backplane. As explained in sub-Chapter 2.5, the front plane contains a structure comprising cells and center objects. The structure center objects are the lenslet centers.

The geometry of cells can take different forms. However, for the sake of simplicity, we will assume here that the shapes of the cells are simple compact polygons that comply with the center object's lattice geometry. Thus, it will be assumed that the cells of a square geometry are squares, the cells of a hexagonal geometry are hexagons, etc. The center object of a cell is the center of its lenslet. The set of all center objects forms a lattice.

The sampling lattice is a projection of the center objects lattice on the backplane, using the viewing point as the projection point.

9.3   The imaging mechanism of a fly-eye sheet

Let us consider a single lenslet placed on a printed image, and let it be observed from a certain viewing point. Two mechanisms generate the image displayed by the lenslet:

1.   Sampling the printed image by the lenslet sampling point,

2.   Expansion of the sampled point graphics to the lenslet aperture.

The sampled graphics in this case are the backplane image function values at the sampling point.

The result of these mechanisms is illustrated in Figure 63. The backplane image in this illustration is a checkerboard pattern. The lenslet is positioned so that its center lies above a common corner of two white and two black squares.

In part (a), the sampling point is located in a white region, the sampled graphics are the color values corresponding to white, and the whole lenslet aperture is white. In part (b), the sampling point is located in a black area, and, correspondingly, the full lenslet aperture displays a black color.

The sampling point's location depends on the viewing point's position. Therefore, the color displayed by the lenslet will depend on the viewer's position.

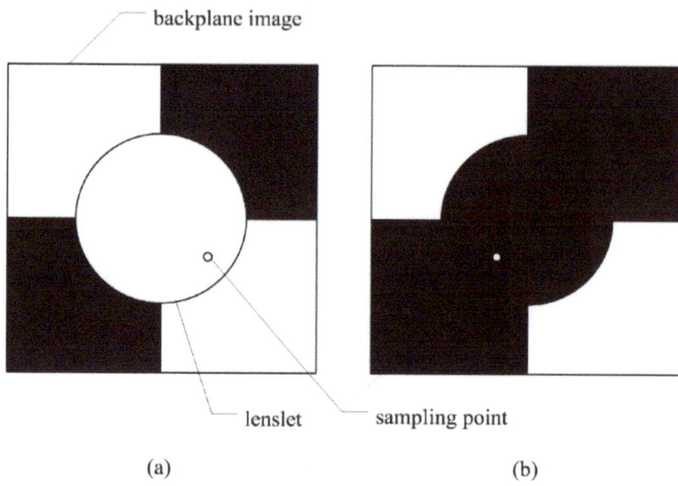

Figure 63:   The optical effect of a lenslet. (a): sampling point in the white region, (b): sampling point in the black region

Figure 64 shows a photograph of a fly-eye sheet superimposed on a thin line. The lenslet's diameter is bigger than the line thickness. Lenslets whose sampling points overlap the line are filled with the line color.

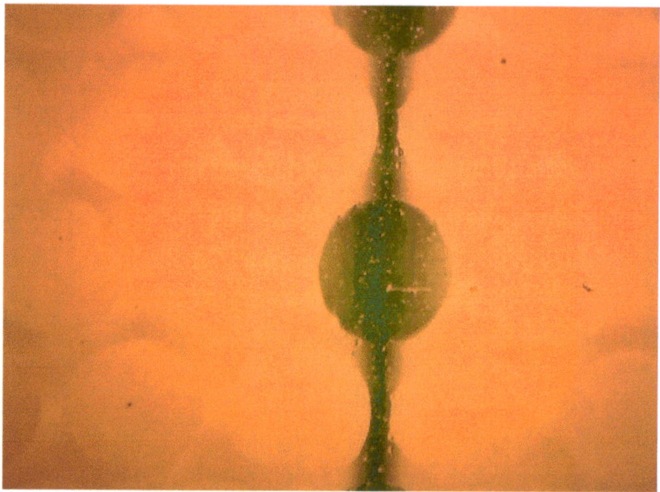

Figure 64:   Fly-eye sheet superimposed on a thin line

9.4   Magnification considerations in projected fly-eye assemblies

The displayed image in 2D projected assemblies was discussed in sub-Chapter 4.4. The magnification considerations are similar to the ones presented for the lenticular case (8.5).

Let p be a certain measure that characterizes the size of the fly-eye cell. Its exact definition is not important; it can, for example, be the average magnitude of the structure's basis vectors. Again, let us assume that the printer's smallest resolved pixel size is p_x. Then, the size of such a pixel in the displayed image is given by (8.1):

$$S = |M| p_x.$$

As explained in 8.4 and 9.3, the smallest resolution element in the displayed image is the characteristic length p. If one wants to display the printed pixels, then the picture must be designed so that

$$S \geq p. \tag{9.1}$$

This sets the following constraint on the magnification value:

$$|M| \geq \gamma p, \tag{9.2}$$

where γ is the printing density corresponding to the pixel size p_x:

$$\gamma = \frac{1}{p_x}$$

The fraction $1/p$ represents the cells density of the fly-eye sheet. Denoting it by l, we write (9.2) as

$$|M| \geq \frac{\gamma}{l}$$

which is identical to the lenticular case analogous constraint (8.4).

Again, analogously to the lenticular assembly discussion in sub-Chapter 8.5 above, the printed pixels become resolved when $|M| > \dfrac{\gamma}{l}$, potentially causing undesired visual effects. The optimal magnification (8.6) avoids these effects and allows picture display at full printed resolution. Consequently, the discussion of the imaging volume presented for the lenticular assembly in sub-Chapter 8.6 is also valid for the fly-eye assembly.

9.5   Example

In this example, we will consider a fly-eye assembly configured to display a 3D moiré surface on a hemi-sphere. The analytical formulas from sub-Chapter 7.9.4 were used to derive the sculpting transformation.

The displayed image in the fly-eye case is a warping of a uniformly magnified version of the primitive image. Since the magnification is uniform, there is no need to design the cell graphics for correct display, as in the lenticular case.

We will use a hexagonal fly-eye sheet for the example. The front plane structure of such a sheet is shown in Figure 65. The cells geometry is characterized by two sizes, f and g. In an ideal hexagonal lattice

$$\frac{g}{f} = \sqrt{3}.$$

This ratio may deviate from this value in real sheets and must be measured to obtain a correctly displayed image.

The sizes f and g determine the lattice's vertical and horizontal cell densities:

$$\text{vertical cell density} = \frac{1}{f},$$

$$\text{horizontal cell density} = \frac{1}{g}.$$

The parameters for this example are given in Table 4, and cell graphics in Figure 66. The sphere was imaged with a 10mm gap above the front surface to avoid the forbidden imaging zone.

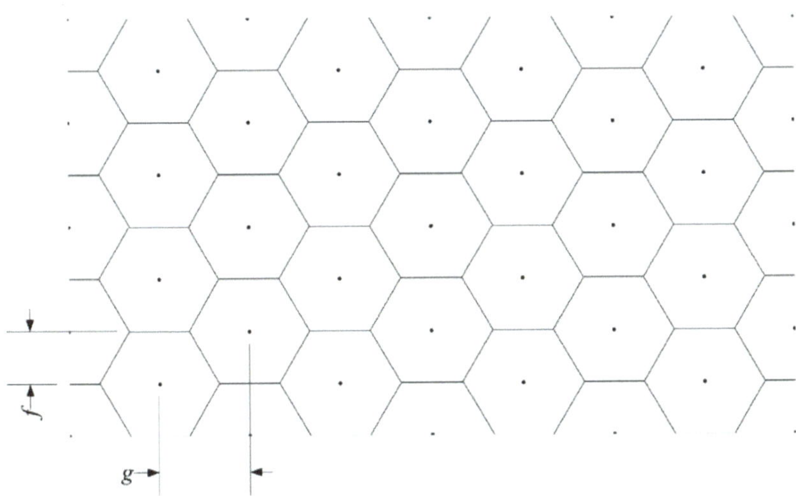

Figure 65: Front plane structure of a hexagonal fly-eye sheet: cells and center objects

Table 4: Picture parameters used in the example

Parameter	Units	Value
Geometry	-	Hexagonal
Assembly width	mm	200
Assembly height	mm	200
Radius	mm	80
Vertical cells density	1/inch	68
Horizontal cells density	1/inch	40
Planes gap	mm	3

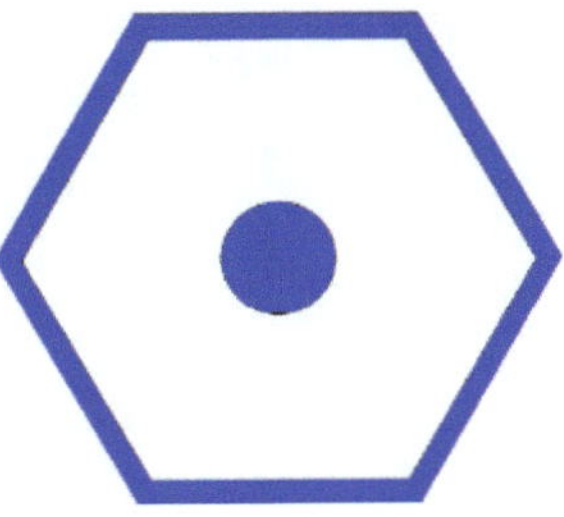

Figure 66: Cell graphics used for the example

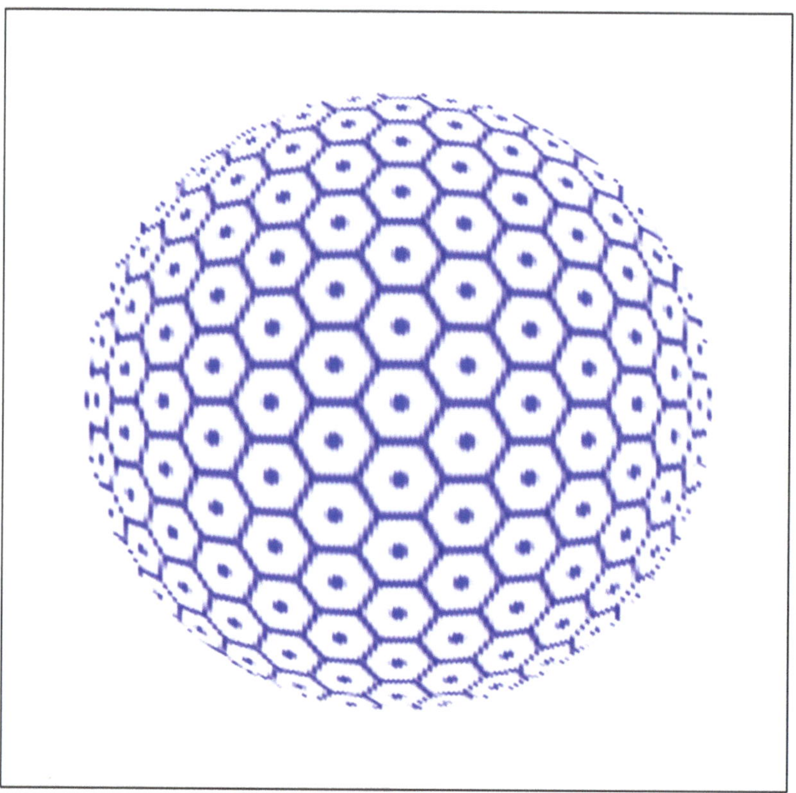

Figure 67: Displayed image for a hemi-spherical surface

10 PARALLAX BARRIER ASSEMBLIES

The parallax barrier assembly uses a material mask in the front plane. In this respect, it is different from optical assemblies, which contain only virtual objects in the front plane. Other than this, Figure 10 applies to parallax barrier (PB) assemblies too.

The mask has openings, or transparent regions, through which the backplane image can be seen. Except for the openings, the mask is made from an opaque material that can be colored or even feature arbitrary graphics. The sampling operation is done simply by obscuration; the viewer can see the backplane image only through the openings in the front plane mask. PB assemblies can be either one-dimensional ("PB1D") or two-dimensional ("PB2D").

The image formation mechanism in PB assemblies is illustrated in Figure 5. The openings in the front plane mask are projected on the backplane. These projections form a sampling mask. The only parts of the background image that the observer can see overlap the sampling mask. One can imagine that the viewable regions of the background image fill the openings of the front mask. The displayed image is the front mask with the openings filled in this manner. Since the sampling mask moves with the viewer's movement, the displayed image will move as well, creating an illusion that it floats in space, just as with the optical assemblies.

In the PB1D case, the openings are equidistant slits. In general, the slits can be curved, but the present formalism can be applied only to straight slits with a constant width. One can define the cells of the PB1D front-plane structure as vertical bands, each band containing a single slit. The center objects are imaginary lines centered with respect to their slits. A scheme of a front plane mask in a 1D assembly is shown in Figure 68. The mask period size is p, and the opening size is s.

In the PB2D case, all openings have identical compact shapes and lie on a two-dimensional lattice. The centers of the openings define a center objects lattice. The cells of the PB2D assembly front-plane structure form a tiling of the front plane, are identical, and each contains a single center object.

In projected PB assemblies, the front plane structure is projected to the backplane exactly as in the optical moiré assemblies. Such a projection creates backplane cells and sampling elements. The sampling elements do not perform actual sampling as in the case of the optical moiré assemblies; therefore, their name is misleading in this context. However, the sampling elements determine the positions of the corresponding sampling mask objects and, therefore, select the image element displayed in their respective front-plane cells. These properties are all that is needed to apply the general formalism for the displayed image in 3D moiré assemblies as described in sub-Chapter 4.2. Moreover, the techniques described in Chapter 6.3 for the sculpting of the moiré surface can be applied to the PB assemblies.

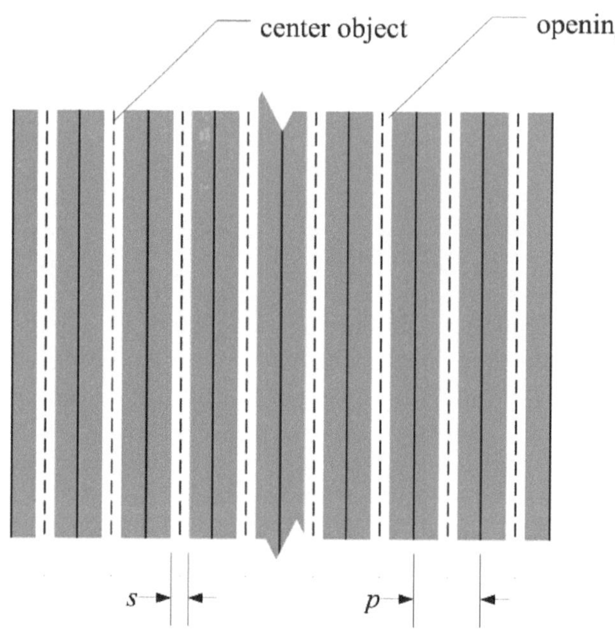

Figure 68: A PB1D assembly mask

We have used the concept of primitive images to create the backplane image in 3D moiré assemblies. In the case of the PB assemblies, the mask itself can serve as a primitive image. This choice is used in the 3D moiré law illustration shown in Figure 6. The shadows cast on the screen (backplane in our terminology) are projections of the mask, also used as a primitive image. This is an example of a projected PB moiré assembly. According to Chapter 4, the displayed image in such assemblies appears on a plane that passes through the assembly projection point, which, in this case, is the point light source.

The PB assembly can be produced without any optical sheets. The mask can be printed or produced mechanically. This simplification comes at a price: very low image resolution. In PB2D assemblies, the effective number of pixels in the displayed cell is given by

$$\text{effective number of pixels} = \frac{\text{cell area}}{\text{opening area}}.$$

Since the front mask can be designed at will, it appears that the number of pixels can be chosen at will too. Unfortunately, in PB assemblies, there is a tradeoff between the brightness of the displayed image and the chosen number of pixels:

$$\text{displayed brightness} = \frac{\text{brightness without mask}}{\text{number of pixels}}.$$

To overcome this, active back-illumination can be used in PB assemblies (Huck, 2002). This tradeoff between optical efficiency and resolution is related to the corresponding tradeoff in a pinhole camera (Pinhole camera, 2023). In this device, the resolution increases as the pinhole diameter decreases. However, optical efficiency decreases as the pinhole diameter decreases. Therefore, the optical efficiency of the pinhole camera decreases when its resolution increases, exactly as in a PB assembly.

In addition to the low optical efficiency, PB assemblies also suffer from low visual efficiency because the displayed image is shown only in a fraction of the cell area: its opening. Low visual efficiency impairs the displayed image quality. The visual efficiency is given by

$$\text{visual efficiency} = \frac{1}{\text{number of pixels}}.$$

So, although the optical efficiency can be boosted by back illumination, there is no way to increase the visual efficiency. For these reasons, it is impractical to design PB assemblies with more than ~10 pixels. For the sake of comparison, both the optical and the visual efficiencies of the lenticular assemblies are 100%. For fly-eye assemblies, these efficiencies are determined by the area fill-ratio of the lenslet apertures. There is no tradeoff between the visual efficiency or brightness and the number of displayed cell pixels in optical assemblies.

A PB1D assembly for displaying a hemi-spherical surface is illustrated in Figure 69, Figure 70, and Figure 71. The front mask was used as a primitive image. In this example, the number of cell pixels in the horizontal direction is 2.

Figure 69:   Front plane mask of the PB1D assembly used in the example

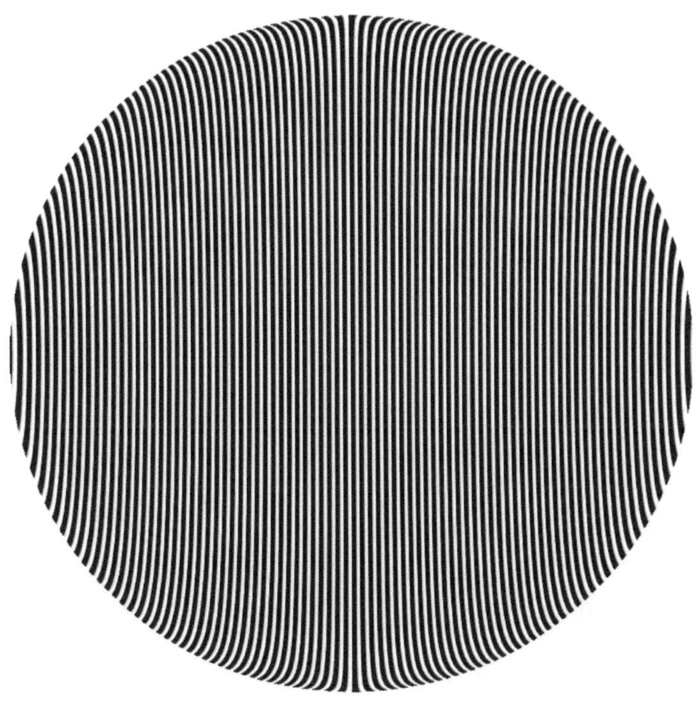

Figure 70: Backplane image warped for a hemi-spherical surface

Figure 71:   View of the displayed image

The displayed backplane resolution in PB assemblies is determined by the front mask, and is typically very low. Therefore, the considerations regarding the imaging volume differ for PB assemblies and are not discussed in this book.

11 MOIRÉ OPTICS

11.1 Changing the assembly gap

In Chapter 6.3, we have described how the displayed image surface can be sculpted by warping the backplane image. However, there is an alternative method to sculpt the displayed image surface: distortion of the backplane from its planar geometry. Such a distorted backplane will be called "back surface."

Suppose that we made a backplane image by projecting a primitive image on a backplane at a distance t_1 from the front plane. According to the discussion in Chapter 14, the displayed image will lie on a surface at a distance H_1 from the front plane, where H_1 is the distance of the assembly projection point from this plane. Assume now that the backplane is translated, together with its image parallel to itself in the z-axis direction to a distance t_2 behind the front plane, as illustrated in Figure 72.

As discussed in sub-Chapter 3.2, the projection transformation depends only on the normalized height h. Since the image on the original and the translated backplanes are identical, the translated backplane image is a projection transformation of the primitive image with the same normalized height. Therefore, its assembly projection point distance from the front plane will be

$$H_2 = ht_2 = \frac{H_1}{t_1} t_2 . \tag{11.1}$$

This is illustrated in Figure 72. This figure shows seven points on the primitive image and their two migrations: first to the original backplane by a projection transformation from H_1, and then to the translated backplane.

According to the discussion in Chapter 1, the displayed image of an assembly with the translated backplane will appear at a distance H_2 from the front plane. Thus, a translation of the backplane causes a translation of the displayed image to a new plane at a distance H_2.

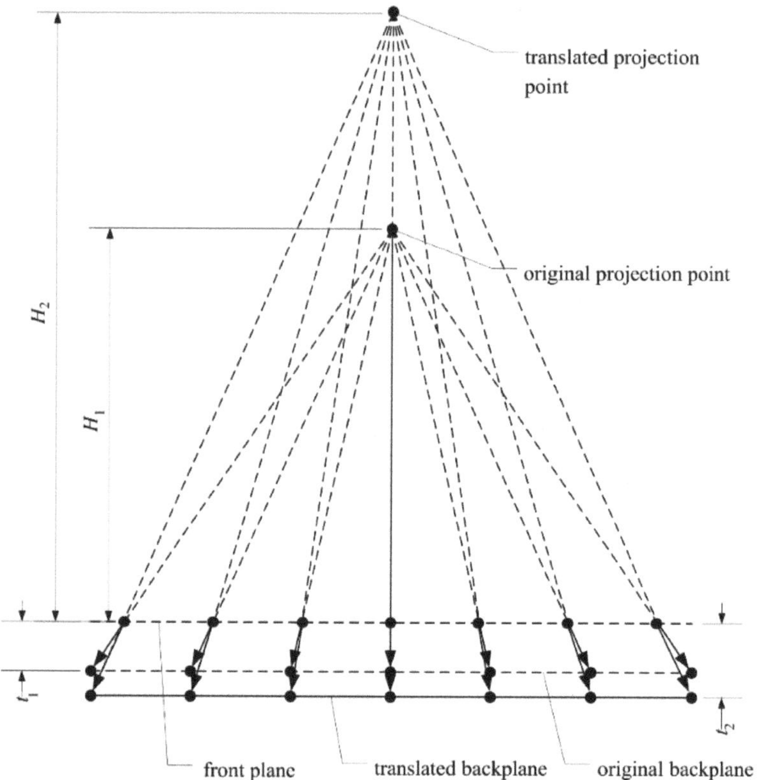

Figure 72: Translation of the backplane with its image

In this construction, the backplane was translated together with its image. Alternatively, one could translate the backplane without the image and derive a new image by a parallel projection of the original backplane image. Parallel projection can be regarded as a perspective projection with a projection point at infinity (Parallel projection, 2023). This transformation is shown in Figure 73.

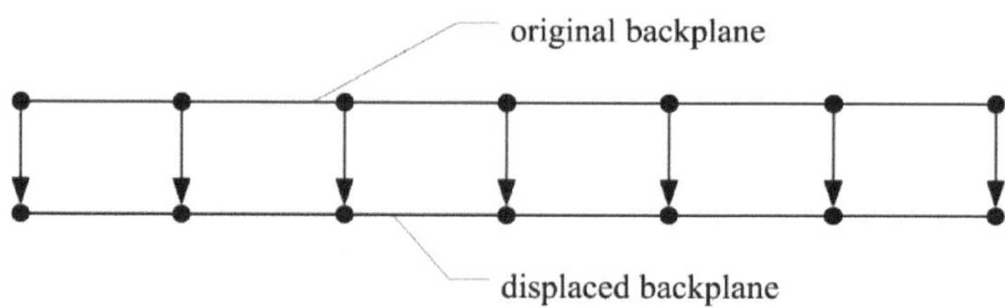

Figure 73: Parallel projection

11.2 Rendering an image on a curved back surface

Let us now generalize the scenario discussed above to a case in which the backplane is displaced and transformed into a general surface. The rendering of the backplane surface image is a texture mapping operation. In the present case, we define this mapping as a parallel projection of a back image onto a specific virtual backplane.

This two-stage rendering is illustrated in Figure 74. The figure shows again seven points picked on the primitive image and then how they are transmitted, first to the virtual backplane and second to the back surface. The arrows connect each primitive image point to its two child points.

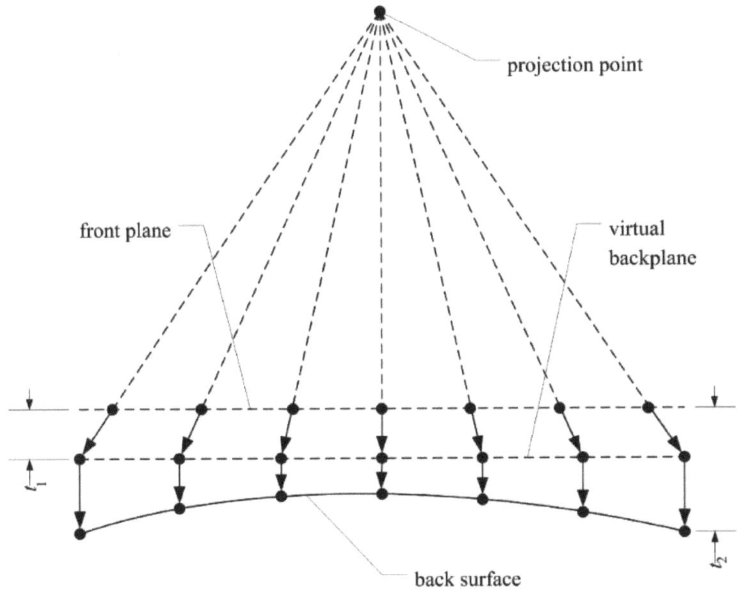

Figure 74: Rendering a back surface image

In this scenario, the height H_2 of the moiré surface depends on the backplane coordinate $\boldsymbol{u}$:

$$H_2\left(\boldsymbol{u}\right) = \frac{H_1}{t_1} t_2\left(\boldsymbol{u}\right) = h t_2\left(\boldsymbol{u}\right).$$

(11.2)

11.3 Moiré optics

The consequences of (11.2) are shown in Figure 75. It is instructive to borrow some concepts from optics to describe this scheme.

We may regard the back and the displayed surface as an object-image pair and the assembly front plane as a unique lens. This lens exhibits two magnifications: one in the z direction and the other in the xy plane. The z magnification is h, and the xy magnification is the moiré magnification. Note that for large viewing distance the magnitudes of these quantities become equal (4.18).

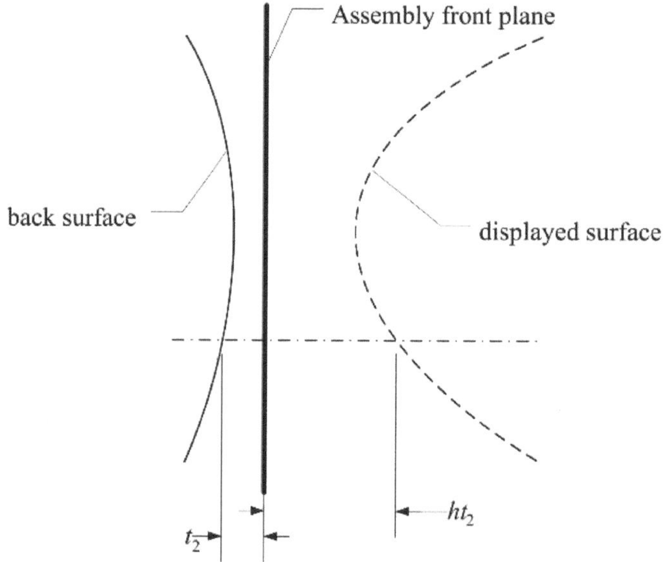

Figure 75: Moiré optics

The z magnification can be chosen at will and can be very large. Therefore, small deformations of the backplane can cause large deformations in the displayed surface.

It is possible to create a back surface with an approximate image by bending the backplane (together with its image). For example, it is possible to wrap it around a cylinder section. If the bending is minor, the back surface image will approximate the projection of the original backplane image, and the displayed surface will be given approximately by (11.2).

In this construction, the warping of the backplane image as described in Chapter 6.3 is replaced by converting the backplane to a general surface. The geometry of this surface can be measured by measuring the parallax of the displayed image with a pair of cameras. This method is different from the common moiré profilometry (Measuring with moiré, 2023).

12 COMPARISON OF 3D MOIRÉ AND LENTICULAR PICTURES

12.1 General

We have demonstrated that the 3D moiré effect can be used to make 3D displays with optical sheets or parallax barrier screens. Any 3D moiré picture with an optical sheet can be mimicked using well-known methods (Integral imaging, 2023; Weissman, Lenticular Imaging, 2018). It is interesting to compare the visual aspects of 3D moiré and conventional displays. Here, we will focus on lenticular moiré assemblies and lenticular 3D pictures. The comparison of fly-eye moiré assemblies and fly-eye 3D pictures follows the same principles, and we leave it to the reader to work it out.

12.2 Infinite-resolution pictures

Let us first consider ideal pictures with infinite resolution. When the lens parameters t and lpi are given, the picture's display is fully determined by the backplane image. Ideal pictures hide many visually important effects, but do reveal the fundamental difference between 3D moiré and conventional 3D pictures.

Lenticular pictures are derived from finite sequences, and, therefore, can display only a finite number of images. This is also the case for our imaginary infinite-resolution pictures. An infinite-resolution 3D moiré picture, on the other hand, displays different images at any two different viewing angles. Since the number of viewing angles is infinite, such a picture will display an infinite number of different views. This implies that it is equivalent to a lenticular picture with an infinite sequence of images. Mathematically, the 3D moiré backplane image $B_{moiré}$ can be regarded as a limit of a series of certain 3D lenticular backplane images B_N.

Let us divide the viewing angle interval into N equal sub-intervals, and let θ_i be the angle at the center of the i-th interval, $i = 1, 2, \ldots, N$, as shown in Figure 76:

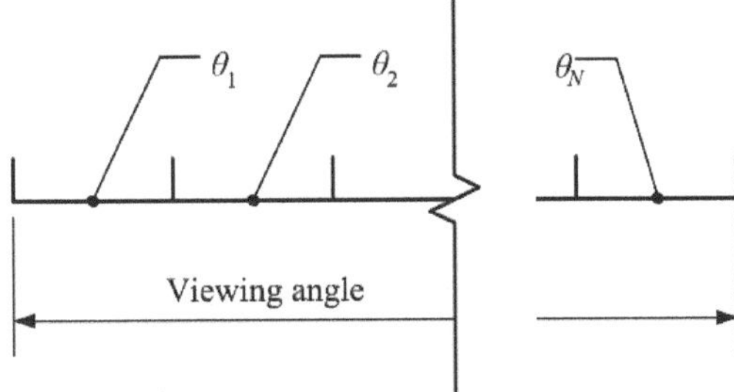

Figure 76: The viewing angles sequence

The moiré assembly can be photographed at the angles θ_i to produce a sequence of images K_i. However, this sequence can also be derived mathematically from $B_{moiré}$ using image processing techniques:

$$K_i = \Gamma\{B_{moiré}, \theta_i\}, \tag{12.1}$$

where Γ is a suitable image-processing operator. This operation may be regarded as "reverse engineering" of the 3D moiré picture. The images K_i form a sequence ϕ_N:

$$\phi_N = \{K_i, i = 1, 2, ..., N\}, \tag{12.2}$$

which can be interlaced (Weissman, Lenticular Imaging, 2018) to produce the N-th backplane image of a 3D lenticular picture:

$$B_N = \Omega\{\phi_N\},$$

where Ω denotes an interlace operator. This operator is adjusted so that when B_N is covered by the same lens as the original moiré picture, it will display the images K_i at the correct size. The 3D moiré backplane image $B_{moiré}$ is the limit of the series B_N:

$$\lim_{N \to \infty} B_N = B_{moiré}. \tag{12.3}$$

Since, for a given lens, the ideal picture's display is wholly determined by the backplane image, one can say that the 3D moiré display is the limit of the displays of the lenticular pictures. Equation (12.3) suggests that the 3D moiré picture can be regarded as a conventional 3D lenticular picture with an infinite sequence. It is well known in the art that pictures displaying greater depth require longer sequences to appear smooth (Weissman, Lenticular Content Editing with Grape 10, 2025; Weissman, Lenticular Imaging, 2018). Since the 3D moiré picture can be regarded as having an infinite sequence, it can display any depth smoothly. This does not imply that the depth display of 3D moiré pictures is unlimited, because the display smoothness is just one of several visual quality factors in 3D displays, although an important one. We discussed some of the other factors in 8.5 and 8.6 above.

12.3   Finite resolution pictures

Real lenticular pictures have finite resolution and, therefore, can display only a finite number of images distinctly. When the sequence length exceeds a certain threshold, the picture displays a blend of several sequence images rather than a single one. This threshold is called "the number of resolvable images," and is denoted by N_r (Weissman, Lenticular Imaging, 2018; Weissman, Lenticular Content Editing with Grape 10, 2025).

For $N > N_r$ the dependence of the picture display on N is reduced, and it diminishes as $N \gg N_r$. Therefore, for real pictures, (12.3) is replaced by

$$B_{N \gg N_r} \approx B_{moiré}.$$ (12.4)

In real lenses, the t and lpi values vary from lens to lens, even within the same production batch, and additional parameters are needed to fully characterize them. In addition, the backplane print depends on the printer; these prints will show differences when printed with different printers, and even with the same printer but with different settings. In this situation, to compare real 3D moiré and 3D lenticular pictures, one has to analyze their displays, and not only their backplane images.

Consideration of the magnitude of the variation in the display of real pictures given the backplane and lens parameters t and lpi is beyond the scope of the present discussion and was not fully investigated. To draw conclusions for real pictures, we must assume that (12.4) holds not only for the backplane images, but also for the corresponding displays:

$$U_{N \gg N_r} \approx U_{moiré},$$ (12.5)

where U is a representation of the picture's display. This equation states that the display of 3D lenticular pictures with sequence lengths far exceeding N_r resembles the corresponding 3D moiré picture's display. However, we do not know whether any noticeable visual differences remain, even for $N \gg N_r$. If there are any differences, the 3D moiré picture's smoothness of display will likely be superior.

12.4 The break line in 3D lenticular pictures

A correctly fabricated lenticular picture displays the sequence images as the viewing point moves horizontally across the picture. A lenticular picture has several angular lobes whose angular extent is the sheet viewing angle (Weissman, Lenticular Imaging, 2018). The viewing angle is an optical property of the lenticular sheet, and in commercial materials it typically ranges from 20° to 60°. The central lobe is called "main," the adjacent lobes are labeled "+1" and "-1", etc. This is illustrated in Figure 77.

A common viewing trajectory is also indicated in Figure 77. A viewer moving on this trajectory will see the lenticular picture images in sequence. The whole sequence is displayed within a single lobe. When the observer crosses the border between two adjacent lobes, the image display restarts. The artist controls only what is displayed in the main lobe. The display in all other lobes is replicated from the main lobe.

An important parameter used for the fabrication of lenticular pictures is the pitch. This parameter determines a viewing distance for which the transition between the lobes is abrupt. In Figure 77 it is assumed that the viewing distance corresponds to the pitch used to fabricate the picture. When the picture is viewed from a different distance, near the borders of the lobes, the viewer sees a discontinuity in the image, in the form of a vertical line called a "break line" (Weissman, Lenticular Imaging, 2018). This break line marks the transition between the last and first images in the sequence as the display restarts. As the viewer crosses the border, the break line sweeps the display horizontally. The break line is a major visual defect in 3D lenticular pictures and limits the viewing space to the vicinity of the distance determined by the picture pitch.

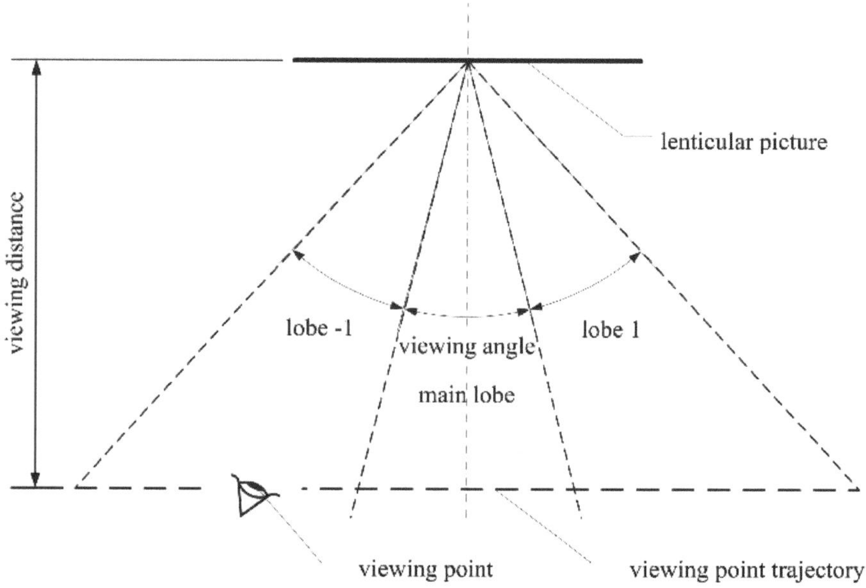

Figure 77: Characteristics of a lenticular picture display

12.5 Break-line-free display

It is known that break lines in 3D lenticular pictures can be eliminated by using special sequences called "cyclic." In cyclic sequences, the first image is also a visual continuation of the sequence. In such a case, the transition from the last to the first sequence image becomes like any other transition, and the break line disappears. Cyclic 3D pictures can display a stunning 3D effect, but their visualization capabilities are limited. In our discussion of infinite-resolution pictures, the sequence ϕ_N (12.2) was cyclic.

The absence of break lines brings an additional advantage: a much higher tolerance to pitch variations. This relieves the necessity to measure the pitch for each lens, as is done in conventional lenticular pictures.

Established methodologies exist for generating cyclic sequences for simple surfaces, such as spheres and cylinders. For example, a cyclic sequence can be obtained by photographing a rotating cylinder with a periodic texture. However, constructing cyclic sequences for more complex surfaces remains challenging, as universal approaches for such geometries have yet to be developed. This limitation constrains the application of cyclic sequences in lenticular imagery and hinders the elimination of break lines.

3D moiré pictures are inherently devoid of break lines and offer uninterrupted display from any viewing distance or angle. The simplicity of achieving a break-line-free presentation with arbitrary surfaces constitutes a unique feature of the 3D moiré technique compared to traditional 3D lenticular imaging methods.

The 3D display of 3D moiré assemblies is pseudo-3D. On the other hand, lenticular pictures featuring geometrically accurate 3D sequences display true 3D views. However, cyclic sequences are generally not geometrically correct, so the lenticular pictures derived from them also exhibit pseudo-3D effects. One can wonder whether it is possible to construct a 3D display that is both break-line-free and true 3D. There is one example fulfilling this: the display of an infinite plane with a periodic texture, parallel to the picture plane. It is presently unknown whether other examples of such displays exist.

13 INDEX

14 REFERENCES

Amidror, I. (2009). *The Theory of the Moiré Phenomenon.* London: Springer-Verlag.

Cox, W. R., Chen, T., & Hayes, D. J. (2001, June). Micro-Optics Fabrication by Ink-Jet Printing. *Optics & Photonics News*, pp. 32-35.

Droptix. (2023). Retrieved from SwissQPrint: https://www.swissqprint.com/ch/en/flatbed-printer/basics/droptix/

Droptix basics. (2022). Retrieved from SwissQPrint: https://www.swissqprint.com/ch/en/flatbed-printer/basics/droptix/

Eaves, R. E. (1974). *USA Patent No. 3,811,213.*

Grapac Japan. (2023). Retrieved from Grapac: https://www.grapac.co.jp/

HALS. (2023). Retrieved from Grapac: https://www.grapac.co.jp/eng_hals/

Huck, J. (2002). *Blog.* Retrieved from Web archive: https://web.archive.org/web/20031227053041/http://pages.sbcglobal.net/joehuck/Pages/more.html#Anchor-53792

Integral imaging. (2023). Retrieved from Wikipedia: https://en.wikipedia.org/wiki/Integral_imaging

Kafri, O., & Glatt, I. (1989). *The Physics of Moiré Metrology.* NY: John Wiley & Sons.

Measuring with moiré. (2023). Retrieved from Cutting Tool Engineering: https://www.ctemag.com/news/articles/measuring-moire

Moiré pattern. (2023). Retrieved from Wikipedia: https://en.wikipedia.org/wiki/Moir%C3%A9_pattern

Nagasaki, K., & Bao, Y. (2008). A 3D display with Variable Depth Moire Pattern. *SICE Annual Conference*, (pp. 1936-1941).

Parallax barrier. (2022, November). Retrieved from Wikipedia: https://en.wikipedia.org/wiki/Parallax_barrier

Parallel projection. (2023). Retrieved from Wikipedia:
       https://en.m.wikipedia.org/wiki/Parallel_projection

Pesach, B. (1997, September 14). THREE DIMENSIONAL DEPTH ILLUSION
       DISPLAY. *application 121760*. Israeli patent office.

Pinhole camera. (2023). Retrieved from Wikipedia:
       https://en.wikipedia.org/wiki/Pinhole_camera

Popims Lens Printer. (2023). Retrieved from lensprinter: https://www.lensprinter.com/

Pratt, W. K. (1991). *Digital Image Processing.* John Wiley & Sons.

Saveljev, V. (2023). *The Geometry of the Moiré Effect in One, Two, and Three
       Dimensions.* Newcastle: Cambridge Scholars Publishing.

Scaling. (2022). Retrieved from Wikipedia:
       https://en.wikipedia.org/wiki/Scaling_(geometry)

Stereoscopy. (2022). Retrieved from Wikipedia:
       https://en.wikipedia.org/wiki/Stereoscopy

Sterescope. (2023). Retrieved from Wikipedia:
       https://en.wikipedia.org/wiki/Stereoscope

SwissQPrint. (2023). Retrieved from SwissQprint: https://www.swissqprint.com/

Tedliashvili, S. (2021). *image 303031004.* Retrieved from Shutterstock:
       shutterstock.com

Tessalation. (2023). Retrieved from Wikipedia:
       https://en.wikipedia.org/wiki/Tessellation#:~:text=A%20tessellation%20or%2
       0tiling%20is,and%20a%20variety%20of%20geometries.

Texture mapping. (2023). Retrieved from Wikipedia:
       https://en.wikipedia.org/wiki/Texture_mapping

Weissman, Y. (2018). *Lenticular Imaging.* Pop3DArt.

Weissman, Y. (2019, November). *The 3D moiré law.* Retrieved from Pop3DArt:
       https://www.pop3dart.com/post/the-3d-moire-law

Weissman, Y. (2025). *Lenticular Content Editing with Grape 10.* Pop3DArt.

Wolberg, G. (1990). *Digital Image Warping.* Los Alamitos: IEEE Computer Society Press.

Dr. Yitzhak Weissman received his Ph.D. degree from Tel Aviv University in 1981. Since then, his career has interleaved scientific and applied research.

During his academic career, Yitzhak published over 30 scientific papers and a book: "Optical Network Theory" in 1991. The subjects of his scientific publications include solid-state physics, quantum mechanics, optical fibers, infrared technology, optical noise, optical engineering, and heat transfer. He spent two sabbatical periods in the US: first in the UC Berkeley Chemistry Department in 1981 as a post-doctoral fellow, and second in the University of Utah Electrical Engineering Department in 1991 as a Visiting Professor.

In 1992, Yitzhak turned to applied R&D and supervised development projects like a flight-control simulator, IR spectroscopy, diamond color grading, and needleless tattooing. He established Advisol in 2001, a company that specialized in polarizing filters for 3D projection displays. These filters were versatile and covered a wide range of applications. Thanks to patented technology, special models of Advisol's polarizing filters reached 70% efficiency in LCD projectors. This breakthrough technology was highly regarded in the field.

In 2010, Yitzhak established Pop3DArt, a subsidiary of Advisol focused on R&D, publication, and software development for lenticular printing and related areas. Pop3DArt published three of Yitzhak's books: "Lenticular Imaging" in 2018, "The 3D Moiré Effect" (the present book) in 2023, and "Lenticular Content Editing with Grape 10" in 2025. Pop3DArt also operates a lenticular print studio.

Yitzhak was born in Poland in 1949. In 1957, he immigrated to Israel with his family. He is married, has two children, and lives in Herzliya, Israel.

9 789655 985207